BOUND BY ICE

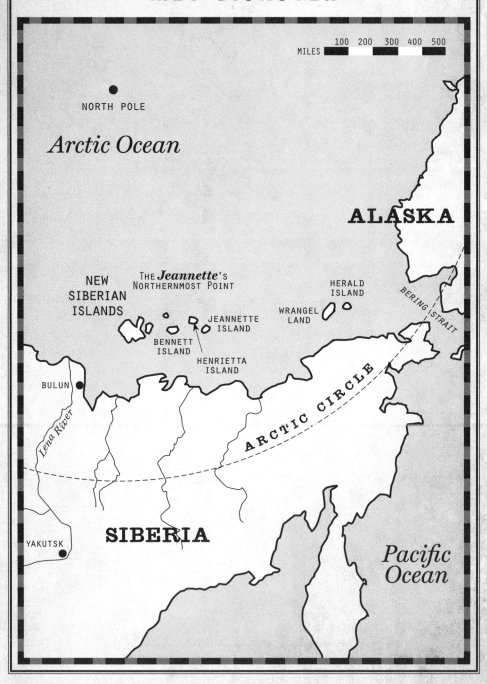

THE REGION WHERE ᴛ̲ʜ̲ᴇ̲ JEANNETTE
MET DISASTER

MILES   100   200   300   400   500

● NORTH POLE

Arctic Ocean

ALASKA

NEW SIBERIAN ISLANDS

The *Jeannette*'s NORTHERNMOST POINT

HERALD ISLAND

WRANGEL LAND

JEANNETTE ISLAND

BENNETT ISLAND

HENRIETTA ISLAND

BERING STRAIT

BULUN ●

Lena River

ARCTIC CIRCLE

SIBERIA

YAKUTSK ●

Pacific Ocean

A True North Pole
Survival Story

BOUND BY ICE

SANDRA NEIL WALLACE AND **RICH WALLACE**

CALKINS CREEK
AN IMPRINT OF ASTRA BOOKS FOR YOUNG READERS
New York

For Alexey and Aneguin, who spoke to the moon

For information about permission to reproduce selections from this book,
please contact permissions@astrapublishinghouse.com.

Calkins Creek
An imprint of Astra Books for Young Readers,
a division of Astra Publishing House
astrapublishinghouse.com
Printed in the United States

ISBN: 978-1-62979-428-0 (hc)
ISBN: 978-1-63592-834-1 (pb)
ISBN: 978-1-62979-915-5 (eBook)
Library of Congress Control Number: 2017937776

First paperback edition, 2022

10 9 8 7 6 5 4 3 2 1

Designed by Red Herring Design
The titles are set in Bullion.
The text is set in Miller Text.

Cover design by Red Herring Design
Front and back jacket: From *The Voyage of the Jeannette: The Ship and
Ice Journals of George W. De Long*, Volume 2, from a design by M. J.
Burns, engraved by George T. Andrew; Anton Ivanov/Shutterstock.com
(ice and water); mycteria/Shutterstock.com (texture in title)

THE OFFICERS AND CREW

OF THE *JEANNETTE*

OFFICERS

Lieutenant Commander George Washington De Long
Lieutenant Charles W. Chipp, *executive officer*
Chief Engineer George W. Melville
Lieutenant John W. Danenhower, *navigator*
Dr. James M. Ambler, *surgeon*
James H. Bartlett, *first-class fireman*
George W. Boyd, *second-class fireman*

SEAMEN

John "Jack" Cole, *boatswain*
Jerome James Collins,
meteorologist
Adolph Dressler
William Dunbar, *ice pilot*
Hans Halmoi Ericksen
Carl August Görtz
Nelse Iversen, *coal heaver*
Peter Edward Johnson
Heinrich Hansen Kaack
Albert George Kuehne
John Lauterbach, *coal heaver*
Herbert W. Leach
Walter Lee, *machinist*
Frank Edward Mansen
Raymond Lee Newcomb,
naturalist and taxidermist

William F.C. Nindemann,
carpenter
Louis Philip Noros
Walter Sharvell, *coal heaver*
Edward Starr
Alfred Sweetman, *carpenter*
Henry Diamond Warren
Henry Wilson

Ah Sam, *cook*
Charles Tong Sing,
steward (cook's assistant)
***Alexey**, *dog driver, hunter,
and trapper*
***Aneguin**, *dog driver, hunter,
and trapper*

*Joined the ship at St. Michael, Alaska

CONTENTS

NORTH OF THE ARCTIC CIRCLE 10

CHAPTER 1: *The Great Unknown* 14

CHAPTER 2: *Longing for the Sea* 21

CHAPTER 3: *The Northern Mystery* 30

CHAPTER 4: *Locked In* 40

CHAPTER 5: *Constant Cravings* 47

CHAPTER 6: *Holiday Spirits* 54

CHAPTER 7: *"Man the Pumps!"* 57

CHAPTER 8: *"Letters to Nowhere"* 63

CHAPTER 9: *First Mates* 67

CHAPTER 10: *A Menacing Encounter* 73

CHAPTER 11: *"Awful Beauty"* 79

CHAPTER 12: *Grinding, Crashing, and Rolling* 86

CHAPTER 13: *Poisoned!* 91

CHAPTER 14: *Catastrophe* 96

CHAPTER 15: *"Superhuman Exertions"* 101

CHAPTER 16: *Off Course* 108

CHAPTER 17: *Lost at Sea* 120

CHAPTER 18: *Cursing Petermann* 125

CHAPTER 19: *A Death March* 130

CHAPTER 20: *Dwindling Company* 141

CHAPTER 21: *"False Hopes"* 145

CHAPTER 22: *"The Siberian Winds"* 152

CHAPTER 23: *Homecoming* 159

EPILOGUE 165

A NOTE FROM THE AUTHORS 170

BIBLIOGRAPHY 173

SOURCE NOTES 177

INDEX 187

PICTURE CREDITS 191

The *Jeannette* is pounded by Arctic ice.

OFF TO THE POLE.

Departure of the Steamer Jeannette from San Francisco.

CALIFORNIA'S HEARTY "GOODBY."

Ten Thousand People Cheer the Gallant Explorers.

THROUGH THE GOLDEN GATE.

Sketches of the Officers and Men of the American Expedition.

JUNE 11, 1881

North of the Arctic Circle

With a sharp *crack* and a fierce shaking of the ship, Lieutenant Commander George W. De Long's worst fear came true. De Long raced up to the *Jeannette*'s deck, gripping the ladder with both hands as it creaked and swayed.

The ship filled with water and listed to one side. Her masts and smokestacks caved in.

The *Jeannette* was going under. There was no way to save her now. If the crew hurried, they could salvage enough food and equipment to sustain them for the nearly impossible journey ahead—five hundred miles across a violently shifting ice pack toward a frozen, inhospitable land.

The thirty-three men were already in poor condition. The *Jeannette* had been frozen fast in the ice of the Arctic Ocean for more than twenty months, and several men were sick or injured. Fresh drinking water was scarce. The men were bitterly cold, always damp, and exhausted.

De Long ordered everyone off the *Jeannette* and waved farewell to it with his cap. The men rested on the ice—

surrounded by dogs, provisions, and equipment—and waited for the ship to sink.

It wasn't a lack of preparation or courage that had put them in this predicament. Like other explorers before them, these men had a never-turn-back attitude. They were seeking the North Pole—a goal that many had tried to reach, but none had ever attained.

De Long knew that his dangerous quest could cost him his life, but he wasn't thinking only of himself. He intended to push human knowledge and achievement to its limits. Maybe there were new islands to be discovered, or unknown species of birds and animals. He'd expected to ride a warm ocean current to the pole. Rumors of a rich, tropical polar sea energized his every thought as he planned the expedition.

But all he'd found was ice.

"Should success crown the efforts of the gallant commander, it will be one of the most brilliant geographical adventures ever won by man. The solution of the Northern mystery would be the event of the nineteenth century."

—The *New York Commercial Advertiser*, July 9, 1879

CHAPTER 1

The Great Unknown

No one had ever seen the North Pole, but the lure of a warm, calm sea at the top of the world had tempted explorers for centuries. Ringed with ice, the sea was said to teem with fish and other sea life, and it might even hold a fertile continent with a lost race of humans or prehistoric animals. Timber, minerals, and other valuable resources waited to be exploited. Any adventurer who could struggle his way to that paradise would soon be famous and rich.

Adventurers imagined a warm, tropical sea at the top of the world.

Many expeditions had tried to conquer the North, usually traveling into the Northwest Passage along the coast of Canada. All were turned back by thick, turbulent ice or sank in the fierce storms of the Arctic. Sailors drowned, starved, or succumbed to diseases like scurvy, pneumonia, and lead poisoning. The best-known and most gruesome of the failed expeditions—led by Sir John Franklin in 1845—ended with the deaths of all 129 men. Some of the crew had resorted to cannibalism, but none survived.

The 1879 voyage of the U.S.S. *Jeannette* was supposed to be different. Better equipped than any previous expedition and with the backing of the U.S. Navy and one of the country's richest businessmen, the launch caused a sensation. James Gordon Bennett Jr.—owner of the *New York Herald* newspaper—funded the voyage and picked George Washington De Long as its captain. News coverage of the preparations and the departure created great excitement and anticipation.

Bennett had a passion for fast boats and racehorses. Tall and lanky, he'd inherited the *Herald* from his father, and his tactics of sensationalizing the news quickly doubled the paper's circulation. He'd publish nearly anything if it would generate a buzz, and he didn't hesitate to cause newsworthy events, or even to make them up. In November 1874, he'd published a story about lions, tigers, and other animals that were killing people in New York City after escaping from the Central Park Zoo. A rhinoceros had gored its keeper to death. People walking in the streets were attacked and mauled.

The entire story was false, but it caused hysteria throughout

George W. De Long

the city. Few people read past the first paragraphs and the headline: "Awful Calamity: The Wild Animals Broken Loose from Central Park." If they'd continued reading most of the story, they'd have been in on the hoax, but Bennett knew that few people would get that far. The article conceded: "Not one word of it is true."

Three years earlier, the *Herald* had caused a sensation with a real news story. Explorer David Livingstone had disappeared in Africa, and Bennett sent reporter Henry Stanley to find him. Stanley wrote exciting accounts of his adventure that were printed in the paper, including the news that he'd found Livingstone.

James Gordon Bennett Jr.

Now Bennett saw an even bigger opportunity for newspaper sales. He'd send an expedition in search of the North Pole and report on it in detail.

The pole was the world's greatest mystery. Americans— still divided from the Civil War—hungered for a ground- breaking discovery. They became obsessed with the pole, the great unknown at the top of the world. England, France, and Germany were planning expeditions to the pole; why couldn't the United States get there first? What better way to unify a country that was still healing from its war wounds?

De Long fit the need for an experienced polar commander.

He'd already piloted a boat through stormy, ice-filled Arctic waters, and Bennett's paper raved about his courage on that mission: "the heroism of Lieutenant De Long and his brave associates must ever remain a sterling tribute of self-sacrifice and devotion in the noble cause so cheerfully undertaken." In 1873, De Long served as second-in-command on the U.S.S. *Juniata*, which set out on a mission in search of a lost ship. The U.S.S. *Polaris* had failed in its attempt to find a route to the North Pole, and the ship and crew were stranded somewhere near Cape York on the northern coast of Greenland.

The *Juniata* went as far north as it could safely go. It carried a smaller, open boat called the *Little Juniata*, and the captain decided that the smaller boat might be better able to navigate the iceberg-filled coastal waters. De Long volunteered to lead nine men on the risky side trip.

De Long cut through narrow passes between islands until ice surrounded the boat and dense fog caused him to lose his way. With no open water in sight, De Long rammed the boat into the ice.

The *Little Juniata* finally broke free but had burned half its fuel and needed to turn back. But Cape York was only forty miles away, and the *Polaris* crew might be there. (De Long had no way of knowing that the men had already been rescued by a Scottish whaling ship.)

A storm "tossed and tumbled" the *Little Juniata*, and huge icebergs threatened to crush it. With his return path rapidly being closed off by the ice, De Long headed back and barely escaped.

"When the gale broke we were in a pitiable condition—hungry, cold, and wet, not a dry thing in the boat," he wrote. "I felt pretty well convinced on two occasions that I was going to leave the bones of our party in the ice."

De Long was also convinced of something else: he would return to the Arctic.

Bennett's *Herald* gushed that De Long's *Little Juniata* excursion "was by far the most daring and brilliant feat of the whole expedition. Bold in conception and masterly in its execution, the plan was such as few would have attempted to carry out. . . . Even when fuel was more than half expended, the gallant commander determined to push ahead, in the very teeth of a furious tempest."

CHAPTER 2

Longing for the Sea

The nail-biting trip on the *Little Juniata* marked the second time George De Long's life had been altered by ice. The first time, a group of teenage schoolmates pummeled him with ice and snowballs.

De Long had spent his childhood in "great seclusion"; his mother wouldn't let him swim, skate, boat, or do just about anything a boy in Brooklyn, New York, would do for fun in the 1850s. She made every effort to "shield him from danger and accident."

George rushed home from school every day, ignoring taunts from other kids. One winter afternoon, those taunts included a bombardment of ice. A chunk hit him squarely in the ear, causing enough damage that he spent the next two months at home.

Restless and longing for freedom, De Long started reading about U.S. Navy heroes from the War of 1812. He wanted that kind of adventurous life for himself, so he applied for an appointment to the U.S. Naval Academy and was accepted. His parents refused to let him go. They offered him three options: become a doctor, a lawyer, or a priest.

De Long was a youthful midshipman at the U.S. Naval Academy when this portrait was taken.

It was easy to convince his squeamish mother that a career in medicine was a bad choice due to "the incessant risks which a doctor ran of contracting a great variety of contagious diseases." The same was true of the priesthood, which demanded contact with the sick and dying.

De Long enrolled in courses at a local college, spending his spare time reading books of adventure to satisfy his "almost uncontrollable longing for the sea." He also started working for a lawyer to see if he'd like that profession for himself.

When the Civil War broke out in 1861, the lawyer joined the Union army. Seventeen-year-old De Long begged his parents to let him accompany his boss. They refused. But when he again asked for permission to enroll in the Naval Academy, they didn't stop him.

De Long graduated from the academy in 1865, shortly after the end of the Civil War. His first assignment was aboard the U.S. Steamer *Canandaigua*. Entering the steerage room that would be his home for the next few years, he was surprised to find that there weren't enough sleeping berths. "To me this seemed altogether wrong," De Long said. "Each midshipman should have his own bunk." Still a naive young man, De Long spoke to some officers about his concern.

"That's right," they told him, recognizing his gullibility. "The thing should be attended to." They sent him to see the admiral.

De Long found the admiral "sitting erect at his desk, making a striking picture with his white hair and sharp black eyes."

Cap in hand, De Long stepped forward and said, "Admiral, I am Midshipman De Long of the *U.S.S. Canandaigua*. Sir, I have been inspecting my quarters on board and I find only two bunks in the steerage for four midshipmen. I came, Sir, to ask you to have two more berths put in before we start."

The admiral's response was blunt. "Well, Midshipman De Long of the *U.S.S. Canandaigua*, I advise you to return on board the *U.S.S. Canandaigua* and consider yourself very lucky that you have any bunks at all in the steerage."

De Long left sheepishly. But the admiral must have admired his grit. He had the two bunks added.

De Long spent three years on the *Canandaigua*, which took him on peaceful missions through the Mediterranean Sea and along the coast of Africa. On a stop in Europe, he met Emma Wotton, the daughter of an American sea captain. Though Emma's father resisted De Long's efforts to court his daughter, seventeen-year-old Emma found De Long "dashing" and admired his "adventurous spirit." She was struck by his grayish-blue eyes and his drooping mustache, which made him appear older than he was.

After just a few short conversations, the love-struck De Long told Emma that "I feel as though I had known you always—as if I had simply been waiting for you to appear." He promptly asked her to marry him, but Captain Wotton insisted on a two-year waiting period. De Long spent most of that time away at sea, worrying that Emma might find someone else to marry. Though Emma had given him a pearl-encrusted gold cross, her enthusiasm for an engagement hadn't matched his. "I had as strong a will as he and was not to be swept off my feet," she admitted.

De Long wrote long letters to Emma while he was away, and eventually her affection grew to match his. They married on March 1, 1871, and Emma gave birth to a daughter, Sylvie, that December. Though voyages kept De Long away from home for long periods of time, Emma was used to absences. "My childhood was dominated by the sea," she said.

So Emma didn't object when James Gordon Bennett Jr. asked De Long to lead a trip to the North Pole. De Long studied the writings of ship captains and scientists, including the esteemed geologist August Petermann, the world's foremost maker of maps. Petermann believed that the warm Pacific Ocean current known as the Kuro Siwo was the key to reaching the pole. He said earlier expeditions had failed because they'd tried to reach the pole via the Atlantic Ocean instead of steaming through the Kuro Siwo.

Emma Wotton De Long   **Sylvie De Long**

Petermann was considered the top authority on the Arctic—even though he'd never been there. One historian described Petermann as an "armchair rover," since he'd hardly traveled anywhere outside his native Germany. Petermann based his theories on the findings of actual explorers, but he often distorted or misinterpreted what he learned. He claimed that the Kuro Siwo passed through the Bering Strait between Alaska and Siberia, working its way under the polar ice ring (or cutting a channel through it) and then warming the northern ocean. "The central area of the Polar regions is more or less free from ice," Petermann insisted in an interview with the *Herald*. He confidently predicted that an expedition could reach the polar sea and return in as little as two months.

Also enticing to Bennett and De Long was the expectation of an unexplored northern continent. Native peoples of Alaska and Siberia told legends about a great land to the north. Russian explorer Baron Ferdinand von Wrangel led several expeditions in the 1820s searching for it but wasn't successful. In 1867, explorers finally glimpsed the southern edge of what became known as Wrangel Land, a large island off the coast of Siberia. With no basis for his claim, Petermann said Wrangel Land was a continent that extended all the way to Greenland.

The next step for De Long was to find a worthy ship. Bennett promised to pay for the ship, the crew, and all provisions, although De Long insisted that the U.S. Navy should have authority over the voyage. It was an arrangement with benefits for him and the Navy: De Long had no desire to give up his naval career, and now he could remain a Navy officer while pursuing his dream of reaching the North Pole. His crew would be subject to military rules and discipline, and he could also select other Navy officers to sail with him. What's more, the Navy would gain valuable knowledge about the northern ocean at little cost.

De Long found a suitable ship named the *Pandora* in England. Bennett purchased the 145-foot steamer, and De Long oversaw repairs in preparation for an Arctic voyage to begin in 1879.

The ship was renamed the *Jeannette*—after Bennett's sister. De Long piloted it on a six-month trip around South America. Strong-willed Emma insisted that she and their seven-year-old daughter make the trip, too.

had no authority under the Act of Congress to appoint these people, but he suggested to me to enlist them as Seamen. This has been done and I have placed opposite their names in my shipping articles rates of pay corresponding to the several capacities of Naturalist, Meteorologist and Ice Pilot.

Upon the receipt of your memorandum from the hands of Paymaster J.W. Kelly, I immediately telegraphed to the Department, asking that proper instructions might be issued, and I am yet awaiting an answer.

Very respectfully,

George W. De Long

Lieutenant, U.S. Navy

Commanding

Arctic Steamer Jeannette
Off San Francisco Cal.
July 2nd 1879

Captain M.P. McCann
U.S. Navy
Commanding U.S.R.S. Independence
Navy Yard, Mare Island

Sir,

In reply to your communication of June 28th I beg to state that upon calling the attention of the Honorable Secretary of the Navy to the fact that I was obliged, in order to get a crew for an Arctic Expedition, to give more pay than Navy pay, and requesting him to give the necessary instructions:— I was informed by him by letter forwarded through the Commandant of the Mare Island Yard, that "the Department does not apprehend that any difficulty will arise in regard to the pay of her crew."

In the particular case you mention, Raymond L. Newcomb though shipped as a Seaman, is the Naturalist of the Expedition. When I applied to the Department for permission to appoint a Naturalist, Meteorologist, and Ice Pilot, I was informed that the Secretary

De Long sent this letter to the secretary of the U.S. Navy while docked in San Francisco, clarifying how the crew would be paid.

The crew included men that were handpicked by Bennett. Alfred Sweetman, from England, was a skilled carpenter who'd worked on Bennett's yachts and proved to be highly reliable. John "Jack" Cole—a short, agile Irishman—was a nimble climber and declared by Bennett to be "worth his weight in gold."

After traveling eighteen thousand miles, the *Jeannette* reached San Francisco two days after Christmas in 1878. Emma later wrote that the voyage with her husband and Sylvie had been "the happiest period of my life."

In a navy yard north of San Francisco, the ship took on larger coal bunkers, new boilers and pumps, new propellers, and a full range of tools, ropes, rifles, compasses, and Petermann's maps and charts. Workers caulked, painted, and fortified the ship with thick lumber to protect it from the inevitable pounding of polar ice.

De Long chose his officers, but he put the hiring of most of the crew in the hands of Lieutenant Charles W. Chipp, the ship's executive officer. Chipp had been with De Long on the *Little Juniata* expedition, and the two men valued each other's experience and friendship.

The hype surrounding the expedition attracted sailors of all types looking for a berth; more than 1,200 applied for twenty-four spots. De Long's orders to Chipp reflected many of the prejudices of the day: "Requirements for crew: Single men perfect health; considerable strength; perfect temperance; cheerfulness; ability to read and write English; prime seamen of course. A musician, if possible. Norwegians,

Swedes, and Danes preferred. Avoid English, Scotch, and Irish. Refuse point blank French, Italians, and Spaniards."

An exception to the no-Irish rule was Jack Cole. Cole, age forty-one, had been working at sea since he was thirteen.

Departure was scheduled for the early summer of 1879.

"Our outfit is simply perfect," De Long told Bennett, "whether for ice navigation, astronomical work, magnetic work, gravity experiments, or collections of Natural History. We have a good crew, good food, and a good ship, and I think we have the right kind of stuff to dare all that man can do."

CHAPTER 3

—▷◆◁—

The Northern Mystery

July 8, 1879: George De Long choked back his emotions. Approaching the *Jeannette* in a small rowboat with his wife, he gazed at Emma, knowing that he wouldn't see her again for at least two years. They'd spoken about the separation constantly, and both ached over it. They knew it was possible that they'd never see each other again.

"I have been thinking," George said to Emma a few nights before, "what a pretty widow you would make."

"I shan't be a widow," Emma replied.

The water of San Francisco Bay sloshed against the rowboat, which was dwarfed by the *Jeannette* and a large fleet of yachts. The oarsmen sculled the boat aside one of the yachts.

De Long, sharply dressed in his full captain's uniform, took his wife's hand. He hesitated, then said simply, "Good-by," and they kissed. Emma stepped onto the yacht and looked back. De Long shook slightly, feeling "as if I had been stunned by a blow," then pulled himself together. In a clear, strong voice, he said, "Pull away, men!"

In De Long's pocket was a small blue bag with a lock of Emma's blonde hair and the cross she'd given him when they first met.

Watching from the *Jeannette*'s deck was George W. Melville, the ship's chief engineer. Melville had worked with De Long on other voyages, and they liked and respected each other. But Melville's life held little of the warmth and affection that was obvious in De Long's relationship with Emma. Melville's marriage was volatile and cold, and he'd spent more than half his adult years on ships, away from his family. His life was the sea, so he was eager for this voyage to begin.

De Long climbed onto the *Jeannette*. A huge crowd had turned out to see it depart. Flying below the American flag on the ship's flagpole was a blue silk flag made by Emma.

"The docks were lined with people—and the Bay was alive with boats of all kinds," De Long wrote. "Telegraph Hill was black with people and crowds were on every dock we passed. Ships dipped their colors to us, people cheered, whistles blew."

Even Bennett's rival newspapers couldn't resist reporting on the voyage. The world was watching.

But the excitement of the day wasn't enough to overcome

Chief engineer George W. Melville

one of De Long's disappointments. No Navy boats were on hand to give the *Jeannette* a patriotic send-off. De Long also fumed about the Navy's last-minute order to search for the *Vega*, a missing Dutch ship, along the Siberian coast. The side trip would cost many precious days and might prevent the *Jeannette* from getting close to the pole that year. Still, it was customary for ships to help each other, even if they were from different countries.

With the voyage finally underway, De Long's mood improved. The *Jeannette* carried an all-star crew, and De Long had confidence in most of his officers.

- De Long had concerns about the navigator, **John W. Danenhower**, who'd once been declared insane and confined to a government hospital. But he'd made the long trip with De Long from England to San Francisco aboard the *Jeannette*, and he appeared to be healthy. Danenhower had a secret, though: he'd contracted an incurable sexually transmitted disease that could cause health problems that would end his Navy career.

- The ship's doctor was **James M. Ambler**, who urged De Long to leave Danenhower off the *Jeannette*, fearing that "he might have a recurrence of his old trouble under the great strain of an Arctic cruise."

- Meteorologist **Jerome Collins** was the *New York Herald*'s representative on the ship and eager to prove himself a proper scientist and reporter. He brought telephone and telegraph equipment, hundreds of feet of copper wire, and sixty experimental electric lights he'd acquired directly from inventor Thomas Edison. Collins expected to light up the ship during the long months of steady darkness, which would close in during November and continue through late January. He also packed photography equipment, but he forgot to take the right chemicals to develop his pictures. (Fortunately, engineer Melville had a workable camera.)

- Shy, quirky **Raymond Lee Newcomb** expected to study the birds and animals of the Arctic. He was more comfortable with birds than with people. Like Collins, he wasn't a member of the Navy. Newcomb was employed by the U.S. Department of Fish and Fisheries. He and Collins were officially appointed as seamen. Because their duties had a scientific nature, De Long planned to treat them both as officers.

- Executive officer **Charles W. Chipp** had been friends with De Long since 1873. He was compact, quiet, and reliable in any crisis.

- Ice pilot **William Dunbar** had extensive experience navigating icy regions of the Arctic and the Antarctic. The oldest crewman at nearly fifty, Dunbar had recently been shipwrecked in the South Pacific, but that didn't deter him from going back to sea.

Ice pilot William Dunbar

The biggest prize was Civil War hero George Melville. The chief engineer was a genius with anything mechanical and could be relied on to fix engines, pumps, stoves, and anything else. The Navy resisted letting him go on the *Jeannette* expedition because he was so valuable elsewhere. De Long insisted that he be included. "He is not only without a superior as an engineer, but he is bright and cheerful to an extraordinary extent," De Long wrote of Melville, whose shock of graying, sandy-red hair circled a shining bald head. "He sings well, is always contented, and brightens everybody by his presence alone."

The heavily loaded *Jeannette* steamed slowly north toward Alaska. Collins and Newcomb—civilians not used to ocean travel—promptly became seasick. So did the cook, Ah Sam. The seasoned crewmen had no problems and happily played musical instruments every night. After he recovered from his seasickness, Collins led the nightly singing and provided music on a small pump organ. But he constantly annoyed Melville, who didn't trust reporters and disliked the Gilbert and Sullivan tunes Collins insisted on singing.

De Long was troubled by more heartfelt matters. After a week at sea, he wrote to tell Emma how deeply he missed her. "I have been remembering something every minute which I would give worlds to have the chance to say." He admitted to being "as lovesick as I was eleven years ago" when they'd met, and he recalled his final glimpse of Emma from the deck of the *Jeannette*. "I could see your handkerchief and answered it by waving my cap as long as I could make out anything at all."

De Long closed the letter with these words: "If by any mischance we should never meet again in this world, be assured that in everything, word and deed, you have always been to me the truest, best and most loving wife that man ever had, and have always cared for me and looked out for me tenderly and lovingly, my precious, precious wife."

In Alaska, De Long loaded up with forty dogs for pulling sleds, six tons of dried fish to feed those dogs, sealskin clothing for the crew, and other supplies. He bought a small porcelain doll for his daughter, Sylvie, and tucked it into the blue pouch with Emma's lock of hair. He mailed the letters he'd written to Emma.

De Long hired two more crew members: bilingual Yup'ik hunters and dogsled drivers from the Native Village of St. Michael. De Long recorded their names as Alexey and Aneguin. ("Alexey" wasn't the man's Yup'ik name; it was a nickname given by non-Native explorers. "Aneguin" was an approximate spelling of that man's Yup'ik name.) Just a few months earlier, Alexey had successfully guided explorer Edward W. Nelson through the Yukon Delta. Alexey and Aneguin would hunt seals, walruses, and bears to provide meat when the *Jeannette* reached the Arctic ice.

The trip to Alaska had been more challenging than expected, as De Long had his first experience with Petermann's inaccurate maps. "Reached this place yesterday afternoon after knocking around for two days in thick fogs among a hundred or more islands, very incorrectly laid down on the chart," De Long wrote from Unalaska Island. "I have seen

In Alaska, De Long mailed this photo and note to Emma along with his letters.

some crooked navigation but our experience in getting through the passes into Behring Sea goes far beyond anything for difficulties."

Instead of heading directly out of Alaska, the *Jeannette* had to wait a week for a coal ship to arrive. De Long needed to refill the bunkers to replace the coal they'd burned on the three-thousand-mile trip from San Francisco. The delay added to his worries that the *Jeannette* wouldn't get far north before winter.

De Long also learned firsthand about another challenge of the Arctic: mosquitoes. "For the last two nights I have hardly had an hour's rest," he wrote to his wife. He lay awake "killing mosquitoes by the dozen. I am one mass of bites from head to foot."

The frustration continued after the *Jeannette* passed through the narrow Bering Strait between Alaska and Siberia. There were no signs of the *Vega* along the Siberian coast. De Long did not believe that the *Vega* was in trouble, since it was equipped for two years in the Arctic, and its captain, Adolf Erik Nordenskjöld, had more experience than any Arctic commander.

De Long was right. The *Vega* had already sailed safely to the south, but the *Jeannette* had traveled hundreds of miles out of its way looking for it. De Long refused to waste more time. He'd fulfilled his orders to execute a thorough search for the *Vega*. Much later in the season than he'd hoped, he got on with the business of exploring. The North Pole was more than a thousand miles away.

The Native Village of St. Michael, Alaska—where skilled hunters Alexey and Aneguin joined the crew

By September 2, De Long estimated that the *Jeannette* was only one hundred miles from Wrangel Land—the land-mass that Petermann said extended all the way to Greenland. Landing there could open the door to nearly unlimited exploration. But ice closed in, and navigation proved difficult in the dense fog. De Long skirted around the ice floes, moving farther from Wrangel, approaching the much smaller Herald Island instead.

His wife later lamented that "he vanished into the Arctic ice and for more than two years was shrouded in mystery."

George W. De Long Journal

SEPTEMBER 4TH, THURSDAY [1879]

We observe a gradual closing in of large floes around us, and a seeming drift of small pieces to the southeast through the small water spaces. The rigging is one mass of snow and frost, presenting a beautiful sight; but as we are more inter-ested in progress than in beautiful sights it has but little charm for us.

SEPTEMBER 5TH, FRIDAY

A clear and pleasant day throughout, with light northerly breeze. At four A. M. spread all fires and got a full head of steam, and entered the pack through the best looking lead in the general direction of Herald Island. For the first two hours we had but little trouble in making our way, but at six A. M.

we commenced to meet young ice ranging from one to two inches in thickness in the leads, and seemingly growing tougher as we proceeded. We ground along, however, scratching, and in places scoring and cutting our doubling, until 8.40 A. M., when we came to pack ice from ten to fifteen feet in thickness, which of course brought us up. Anchored to the floe to wait for an opening.

LIEUTENANT JOHN W. DANENHOWER, NAVIGATOR:

While working along the pack the captain, the ice pilot, or myself, was always in the crow's-nest. The crow's-nest of the *Jeannette* may be described as a large cask, having a trap-door in the bottom, through which the observer entered. It was then closed and formed a floor on which he stood. The crow's-nest was secured by iron bands to the foretop-gallant mast, above the topmast cross-trees. It was made of wood and was about 5 feet in height and 4 [feet] in diameter at the base and 3 at the top. There was a little ridge where a person could sit. There were places for putting glasses, the long glass, and the binoculars. We coasted the pack until September 6.

On an earlier trip to the Arctic, the *Jeannette* (then called the *Pandora*) was also trapped by ice.

CHAPTER 4

Locked In

De Long was shocked by how quickly the ice had surrounded his ship. It spread in every direction—more than ten feet thick and growing thicker as the small pools on the ice's surface froze. The *Jeannette* was frustratingly close to Herald Island—De Long could clearly see it in the distance—but reaching the island with the ship was impossible as long as the ice held them captive.

"As far as the eye can range is ice, and not only does it look as if it had never broken up and become water, but it also looks as if it never would," De Long noted on September 6. His plan to spend the winter on Herald Island was slipping away as quickly as the ice froze. He hoped a huge burst of wind might shatter the ice pack and leave a narrow channel.

"This is a glorious country to learn patience in," De Long grumbled. If he hadn't wasted time looking for the *Vega*, he certainly would have made it to Herald Island or farther. Instead, he faced a long winter in the ice.

Pressure from the squeezing pack caused the ship to groan as two giant ice floes crashed together. The ship leaned over toward its starboard side, and it moved farther from Herald Island by the hour. "The whole pack, with ourselves fast in it, is evidently drifting," De Long wrote.

Could a dogsled make it across the ice to Herald Island and return safely? A quick exploration of the island would at least add some new knowledge and partly make up for the sudden halt of the expedition. "It is unpleasant to realize that our exploration for a whole year should come to a stop on the 6th September," De Long wrote. "While waiting for next summer we are consuming our provisions and fuel, and running the risk of the enfeeblement of the general health which a winter's confinement may produce."

De Long chose executive officer Chipp to lead chief engineer Melville, ice pilot Dunbar, and Yup'ik hunter Alexey on the dangerous trip over the ice. They'd be helped by eight dogs pulling a sled with enough food for a week.

"It was thought that the ice closed in on Herald Island," Melville explained. They trekked to within a few miles of the island but were stopped by wide lanes of open water. "It would have been sheer folly to await the freezing of the water and then make a dash for the foot of the precipitous rocks, without the aid of a boat."

Even if the *Jeannette* had been able to reach the island, the crew's situation wouldn't have improved. Chipp saw no place to anchor that would offer any protection to a ship. The island looked rocky and barren. Spending the winter there was not an option. The crew was better off on the *Jeannette*.

The group turned back, horrified to see the ship drifting rapidly away from them. If they didn't make good time, they'd be left to starve and freeze to death. They zigzagged along the edges of open water and climbed over towering piles of ice. They lost sight of the *Jeannette* at times but finally reached it.

Chipp reported to De Long that he had seen "no driftwood, but sighted many bear-tracks, and one raven." Alexey shot a young seal and dragged it to the ship.

"Herald Island will be of no use to us, even if we could get to it," De Long wrote, "but we daily seem to be increasing our distance from it by drifting to the N. W."

Lieutenant Charles W. Chipp

Seals provided fresh meat for the crew—a change of pace from canned provisions.

De Long and the crew settled in for a frustrating winter, hunting polar bears and seals (which they called "floe rats"), taking measurements of the latitude and longitude, recording the wind speed and air temperature (which consistently stayed well below zero), worrying about how much coal they were burning, and preparing for an escape if the ship sank.

On September 19, De Long reported that Herald Island "is very distant." The *Jeannette* could not be budged, and its crew would spend the winter drifting wherever the ice took them on its northern spiral. "We are securely held as in a vise."

JOHN W. DANENHOWER:

Our position was not an enviable one. At any moment the vessel was liable to be crushed like an eggshell among this enormous mass of ice. . . . We heard distant thundering of the heavy masses, which threw up high ridges of young ice that looked like immense pieces of crushed sugar.

George W. De Long Journal

OCTOBER 3D, FRIDAY

At three P. M. we were startled into activity by the report of "A bear on the ice close to the ship!" Five or six of us immediately went in pursuit, spreading out to inclose the bear should he allow it. He had a long start, however, and most of us gave up the chase after a mile or two. Mr. Newcomb, Aneguin, and Alexey kept on, and at 5.20 Aneguin came back with the pleasant news that the bear had been overtaken and killed. Melville and I took a couple of sleds and teams and some men, and brought back the prize—a female bear, weighing, I should judge, about 500 pounds. The captors had already skinned and cut up the carcass, so we could not weigh it.

Men and dogs haul a polar bear back to the *Jeannette* after a successful hunt.

OCTOBER 5TH, SUNDAY

At ten A. M. read the Articles for the Government of the Navy [a written order designed to maintain military discipline], and mustered the crew. Everybody seemed in excellent health and spirits, and nothing disheartened by our being thus early beset and the almost absolute certainty of our wintering in the pack. The forecastle [crew's quarters] was dry, warm, and comfortable. . . . In the cabin the air is good enough, except at night, when the wretched Walton lamp smokes so as to fill it. Melville has made a tin pipe four inches in diameter, perforated it with half-inch holes, and fitted it into the skylight cover, and this works well without depriving us of light.

OCTOBER 17TH, FRIDAY

We have now seven seals hanging in the rigging, which will in turn serve for as many dinners, while their own blubber may serve to cook them.

Walruses provided food for men and dogs.

Raymond Newcomb Journal

[Alexey] and myself got two walruses; both had fine tusks. . . . Their combined weight was some 3,600 pounds. The Indian bared one arm, and pushed it down the throat of the one he shot, and pulling it out wiped the fresh blood on his forehead, after this applying some snow on the place. This he said was for 'good luck,' and 'because his father taught it him.'

Though Newcomb was fascinated by the Yup'ik rituals, he incorrectly identified Alexey and Aneguin as Indians.

CHAPTER 5

Constant Cravings

R aymond Newcomb groaned in his sleep, his mouth watering. Pumpkin pie. Just one slice. That was his overwhelming desire—so strong that he constantly dreamed about it. He'd eaten so much of it while growing up in Salem, Massachusetts.

Newcomb shook himself awake. Moisture clung to every surface of his cold, damp cabin. How he wished for a tasty relief from his craving. "Visions of pie—pumpkin pie, the particular weakness of a New England Yankee—always occupied an aggravatingly prominent place," he explained.

There would be no pie. The day's meals would be the same as yesterday's. And tomorrow's.

As they sat down to eat, other crewmen shared fond memories of their favorite foods, too. After months aboard the *Jeannette*, the sameness of their diet had the men craving fresh fruit, pastries, and

Raymond Newcomb

other delicacies. Even the occasional tastes of a freshly killed seal's liver or a bear's tongue were welcome variations.

It was no different among the officers. De Long craved fried oysters, while Melville and Dr. Ambler laughed about eating an entire duck or a turkey or a goose. Chipp joked that they should all be satisfied with "a ten-cent plate of hash."

The men were well nourished, just bored with the food. De Long declared that the meals were "superior to any previous Arctic experience" in both quality and quantity. He kept a detailed list of the food prepared and served by the cooks.

The meals varied slightly from day to day, but the menus were usually repeated every week. Typical meals for the thirty-three men looked like this, with many of the items coming from cans:

Breakfast	Dinner [SERVED MIDDAY]	Supper
Beef	Bear meat	Mutton
Potatoes	Soup	Ham
Fresh bread	Pork	Potatoes
Butter	Canned tomatoes	Peach butter
Coffee	Corn	Dried apples
Sugar	Potatoes	Butter
	Hard bread	Sugar
		Tea
		Milk
		Bread

Although the food on the *Jeannette* seemed dull, there was plenty of it. Water for drinking, however, caused constant concerns. De Long assumed that the crew could simply thaw chunks of ice, relying on August Petermann's statement that "beginning at a certain thickness the ice is almost free of salt." That proved to be a near-fatal mistake. Every bit of ice they tested contained unhealthy levels of salt. Though the ship had started out with many barrels of fresh water, it wasn't meant to last for more than a few months.

The men suffered dehydration and diarrhea from the salty water, and they ran the risk of scurvy—a disease common to sailors. Scurvy is caused by a lack of vitamin C, which is found in citrus fruits and some vegetables. The crew of the *Jeannette* drank lime juice daily to prevent the disease, but too much salt in the diet can limit the absorption of C and other vitamins.

The *Jeannette* carried equipment to purify saltwater, but distilling required huge amounts of coal to fuel the boilers. "As coal is the most precious article which we have on board ship, its economical use is a matter of paramount importance," De Long wrote.

But there was no choice. Without fresh water, they would die. The crew needed at least forty gallons a day for cooking and drinking.

The distilling was inconsistent and inefficient. Some days the water tasted fine; other days it was undrinkable. De Long turned to Melville for a solution, and the chief engineer improved the situation immensely by reducing the amount of saltwater that slopped from the holding tank into the distilled water.

"Melville has made a complete success of the distiller, and now we get our water pure," De Long wrote. That solved one issue. "But it takes two pounds of coal for every gallon of water, and that expenditure will ruin us if we have to keep it up. Snow, snow is what we want."

Finally, a driving snow piled up. Overjoyed, De Long "scooped up two handfuls of it and had the surgeon test it; but alas! even newly fallen snow had, in being driven across the face of the floe, caught up and carried along too much salt. I shall soon believe that it drops salt from the sky."

There was no option but to continue distilling every drop.

As the months wore on, certain food items simply ran out or began to rot. The sameness of the meals magnified the boredom. "There can be no greater wear and tear on a man's mind than this life in the pack," De Long wrote. "All our books are read, our stories related; our games of chess, cards, and checkers long since discontinued."

The only one not bored was Raymond Newcomb, who overcame the monotony with those dreams of pumpkin pie and an intense focus on his work as the ship's taxidermist and naturalist. Quiet, serious, and always busy, he'd earned the nickname "Ninkum." He took it in stride when others poked fun at him for constantly chasing after the creatures of the Arctic.

"Here, Ninky, quick!" called one officer on sighting a large bird. "Come catch a goose!" Newcomb caught the bird—an albatross—then skinned and mounted it.

Newcomb recorded precise details about the birds and animals he studied. After shooting two Ross's gulls, he described the birds as "very buoyant and graceful on the wing, beautiful pearl blue on the backs, vermilion feet and legs, and lovely tea rose on the breasts and under parts, the rosy tint being scarcely a color, yet blending in exquisite harmony with the pearl blue of the upper parts."

One day, Newcomb caught nine mosquitoes. "These were the first entomological specimens collected after we entered the Arctic Circle," he noted with pride. That same day, he added a fly and a spider to the collection.

De Long admired Newcomb's ability to track down foxes, birds, and even insects. "Natural History is well looked out for," the captain wrote. "Any animal or bird that comes near the ship does so at the peril of its life."

De Long's admiration had its limits, though. The dissected creatures Newcomb kept in his quarters began to stink, and other crew members complained. Finally, De Long couldn't stand the smell for another minute. He gave Newcomb an order: "Remove those birds!"

Newcomb reluctantly got rid of the worst-smelling specimens.

They made a good meal for the dogs.

Newcomb sketched the Arctic wildlife, including this Ross's gull.

The Jeannette's Winter Schedule,

1879–1880

ISSUED BY GEORGE W. DE LONG

---

6 A.M.	*Call executive officer.*
7	*Call ship's cook.*
8.30	*Call all hands.*
9	*Breakfast by watches.*
10	*Turn to, clear fire-hole of ice, fill barrels with snow, clean up decks.*
11	*Clear forecastle. All hands take exercise on the ice.*
11.30	*Inspection by executive officer.*
12 n.	*Get soundings.*
1 P.M.	*One watch may go below.*
2	*Fill barrels with snow. Clear fire-hole of ice.*
3	*Dinner by watches.*
4	*Galley fires out. Carpenter and boatswain report departments to executive officer.*
7.30	*Supper by watches.*
10	*Pipe down. Noise and smoking to cease in forecastle, and all lights to be put out, except one burner of bulkhead lantern. Man on watch report to the executive. During the night the anchor watch will examine fires and lights every half hour, and see that there is no danger from fire.*

Raymond Newcomb Journal

NOVEMBER 7

Ice is in motion as yesterday, cracking fearfully. . . . Great pieces are pushed about like toys. . . . Have gun and knapsack ready to leave at a moment's notice for—God knows where.

George W. De Long Journal

DECEMBER 4TH, THURSDAY

Were it not for our daily walking exercise of two hours I fear we should stagnate. From eleven A. M. to one P. M., however, all hands are sent out of the ship. The officers generally walk, and the men go hunting . . . or kick foot-balls. We have a fine, level, smooth place, two hundred and forty yards in length, to walk on, and we manage to put in from four to six miles in the two hours.

DECEMBER 9TH, TUESDAY

The necessary and inevitable refuse of the ship has rendered our surroundings not at all pleasant to contemplate. If we could only have snow, this might be covered and kept out of sight, but I begin to believe snow never falls here.

DECEMBER 25TH, THURSDAY

Christmas Day! This is the dreariest day I have ever experienced in my life, and it is certainly passed in the dreariest part of the world. And yet we (or rather I) ought not to complain, for it is something to have had no serious mishap up to this time.

CHAPTER 6

Holiday Spirits

fter writing that gloomy journal entry on Christmas Day, De Long was surprised when Jack Cole visited him in his cabin. Cole invited the captain and the other officers to the deckhouse for a holiday celebration. De Long later wrote that the crew played music and sang songs, "and Alexey gave us a native dance." The captain wasn't cheered by the performances, but he admitted that "the crew seemed to have a merry Christmas."

De Long's spirits improved a week later, when the crew's New Year celebration took place under a shining moon with a blood-red halo. After a dinner of "Arctic turkey" (roasted seal), macaroni and cheese with canned tomatoes, and plum pudding, the crew staged a performance with music and storytelling. "Our men had rallied from their failure to get up one for Christmas, and seemed determined to make this entertainment good enough for both occasions," De Long wrote.

The crew had constructed a small stage, decorated with flags. A minstrel show began, with "jokes and conundrums sandwiching in with the songs. . . . [Alfred] Sweetman's songs were very good, and [Albert] Kuehne's violin solo was fine indeed, especially when one takes into consideration the fact that a seaman's life does not serve to render the fingers supple and delicate."

Jack Cole drew on his Irish roots to dance a jig "with all the gravity of a judge," and Alexey and Aneguin performed Yup'ik dances.

Jerome Collins—the *Herald* reporter who was not well ac-cepted by many of the men— redeemed himself for one night by reciting a lengthy and humorous

Meteorologist Jerome Collins accomplished little on the *Jeannette*, but he was an energetic entertainer.

poem he'd written "in which each one of the crew was made the subject of a rhyme in turn."

Short skits rounded out the evening. "When, the perfor-mance over," De Long wrote, "we broke up at eleven o'clock, we all felt satisfied alike with the ship, the minstrels, ourselves, and the manner in which we had celebrated the first day of the year of our Lord 1880."

Raymond Newcomb Journal

One day soon after New Year's I was out walking with one of the Indians. Noticing the new moon he stopped, faced it and, blowing out his breath, he spoke to it, invoking success in hunting. . . . [Alexey] told me this particular manner of invoking good will was a secret handed down to him by his father, who got it from a very old Indian.

George W. De Long Journal

JANUARY 5TH, MONDAY

This morning the doctor came to me and represented that Danenhower's case was of a very serious character, and that there was great danger of his losing the sight of his left eye. Owing to the necessity for shielding the eye from all light, it would become necessary for Mr. Danenhower to remain in his room in total darkness, and it was feared that this might affect his general health and depress his spirits. I am much distressed at the news, for Danenhower is highly prized by all of us, and by his efforts has kept us many an hour from moping. He is now shut out from all participation with what is going on, and we can do nothing but go down occasionally and sit with him in the dark and talk with him. He is cheerful enough himself, however, and, having great force of character, has made up his mind to accept the situation and fight it out patiently.

JANUARY 13TH, TUESDAY

The carpenters commenced to-day the building of two more sleds, to carry our cutters [large rowboats] in case we have to abandon the ship, which God forbid.

CHAPTER 7

"Man the Pumps!"

Captain De Long never rested easy. Long after midnight, on January 19, he sat in his quarters, perhaps thinking ahead to the following summer, when the *Jeannette* might finally break free from the ice. Summer seemed a long way off—the sun hadn't risen above the horizon for more than two months in what seemed like an endless, dark winter.

In the back of the captain's mind, as always, was a nagging awareness that the ship might crash to the bottom of the ocean before summer came. The ice had been relatively quiet lately, "but this horrible uncertainty grows wearisome."

De Long grimaced as a familiar loud noise rocked the ship. "I know of no sound on shore that can be compared to it," he wrote. "A rumble, a shriek, a groan, and a crash of a falling house all combined might serve to convey an idea of the noise with which this motion of ice-floes is accompanied."

The new assault sounded like the cracking of the ship's frame. De Long rushed to the deck to find the cause of the noise, but all seemed calm. "The ice was perfectly quiet, and no evidence of anything wrong could be found about the ship." So he went to bed.

By morning, the ice was "groaning and grinding," squeezing the ship and piling up around it and under it. But the crew didn't worry about the potential danger. They rushed out onto the giant blocks of ice like excited kids. "With light hearts the men dispersed themselves upon the ice," Melville wrote, "climbing the slopes of the marble-like basin, leaping from block to block, clambering up pinnacles and tumbling down with laughter . . . all hailing and shouting in boyish glee,— when, suddenly, the dread cry of 'Man the pumps!' put a check to their short-lived sport, and sent every one scudding back."

Two inch-wide streams of water flowed into the *Jeannette*'s bilges, and the water was already three feet deep in places.

The ship was equipped with several pumps, but only one worked. Crew members hustled to move flour and other provisions from the storeroom, and others used hand pumps to try to keep ahead of the leaks. William Nindemann, one of the ship's carpenters, led the way, working frantically in the icy water.

"The temperature at this time was about 40° Fahrenheit below zero, and as the water rushed into the hold it almost instantly froze," Melville wrote. "Pouring steadily in, it crept above the fire-room floor, and fears were entertained that it might reach the boiler furnaces before the steam-pumps could be started."

Men slogged water from the hold in a barrel. "Time meant life or death," Melville warned.

Pumping and hauling the water wasn't enough. The leak had to be slowed. Nindemann stood in knee-deep water, filling the cracks with oakum and tallow. "As fast as he stuffed it in below the water came out above," De Long wrote. Nindemann never seemed to tire or feel pain, and the captain called him "as hard-working as a horse." With the *Jeannette* in danger of sinking, he and fellow carpenter Alfred Sweetman didn't rest for days.

Melville went to work to repair a steam-powered pump, "for men cannot stand pumping from now till spring." He succeeded, working around the clock while others packed sledges with food, sleeping bags, and other supplies in the expectation that they might soon abandon the ship.

By hand and by steam, the pumps rid the ship of 3,300 gallons of ice-cold seawater per hour. But that only kept the water from getting deeper. Nindemann and Sweetman patched with plaster of Paris and ashes.

"We do not gain much on the water," De Long wrote, "but then the water does not gain on us." He made a notation in his journal to recommend Nindemann and Sweetman for Congressional Medals of Honor for their bravery and unending hard work.

De Long knew that the situation could not continue. "Pumping by hand will use up my crew, and should we be obliged to leave the ship in a sudden smash-up, I would have an exhausted body of men to lead over the ice two hundred miles to a settlement. If the water freezes in the ship, more damage may be done in a day than we could repair in a month."

Fortunately, the repairs worked. A week after the leak began, Melville calculated that they'd reduced the flow to 2,250 gallons per hour. With the steam pump working full blast, the hand-pumpers could take some breaks. But it took fuel to fire the steam pump, reducing the coal supply by a worrisome amount.

The slowing of the leak was not the only welcome news. On January 26, De Long recorded "the reappearance of the sun!" for the first time in seventy-one days. "Although the glare was trying to the eyes, making me blink like an owl at first, I could not get enough of the pleasant sight."

Melville rigged up another pump, but its engine wasn't powerful enough to make much difference. So he adjusted the pump with melted tin and a pair of plungers. The new scheme worked, and it took some of the pressure off the boilers.

"At last we have succeeded in reducing our fearful expenditure of fuel to a reasonable amount; 400 pounds of coal a day will now run our two steam-pumps, and that is much more comforting than burning 1,000 to 1,200 in the main boiler furnaces," De Long wrote. Melville also built a windmill that helped power the pumps. Still, they used much more coal than expected.

"Verily, all our troubles are coming upon us at once," De Long complained, listing among those troubles the fact that Danenhower's eye condition was rapidly declining. This forced

**William Nindemann,
ship's carpenter**

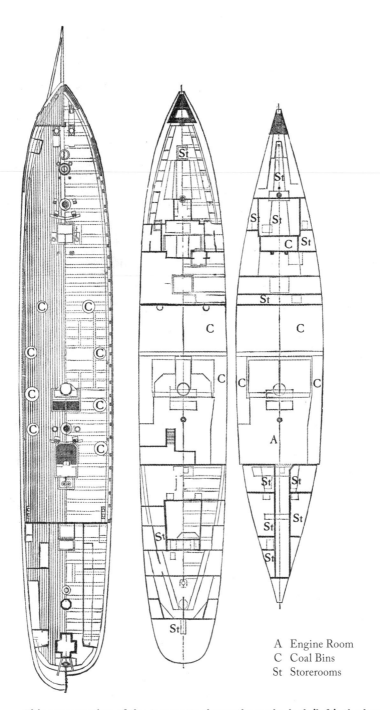

A Engine Room
C Coal Bins
St Storerooms

This cross section of the *Jeannette* shows the main deck (left), the berth deck (middle), and the hold (right). Flooding occurred primarily in the hold, including the engine room (A), coal bins (C), and storerooms (St).

Dr. Ambler to probe and cut to relieve the pressure in the eye and ease the constant flow of pus. Ambler suspected that Danenhower suffered from sexually transmitted syphilis, which could also explain his past history of mental illness.

Also, Jerome Collins, James Gordon Bennett's reporter, had turned out to be combative and inept and was always in De Long's doghouse. None of the lighting or

Lieutenant
John Danenhower

telegraph equipment he'd brought on board had worked, so he'd sent no reports to the *Herald* after leaving Alaska. Collins also refused to exercise or pay attention to De Long's orders. He annoyed the other men with his constant puns. (Why won't the *Jeannette* ever run out of fuel? Because we have Cole on board!)

Overall, every inch of the ship was "wretchedly wet and uncomfortable." Worse, from De Long's point of view, was the distress of accomplishing little to advance science or navigation. He came to the sickening conclusion that the leaks would prevent the *Jeannette* from reaching the North Pole. "All our hoped for explorations, and perhaps discoveries this coming summer, seem slipping away from us, and we seem to have nothing ahead of us but taking a leaking ship to the United States."

CHAPTER 8

"Letters to Nowhere"

With no word from the *Jeannette* for many months, newspapers at home speculated that the crew was either thriving in the Arctic or had met with disaster. Bennett's paper put the best possible light on things. In a *Herald* article headlined "Arctic Exploration: No Reasons for Apprehensions," the famous explorer Isaac Hayes wrote with certainty that the *Jeannette* would return safely with "triumphant news." Hayes had once been icebound in the Arctic on an earlier search for a route to the North Pole, so his words assured some readers. But other newspapers predicted doom.

Famed explorer Isaac Hayes assured *New York Herald* readers that the *Jeannette* was not in trouble.

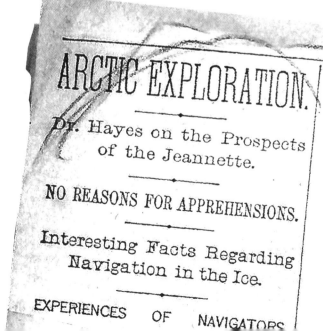

ARCTIC EXPLORATION.

Dr. Hayes on the Prospects of the Jeannette.

NO REASONS FOR APPREHENSIONS.

Interesting Facts Regarding Navigation in the Ice.

EXPERIENCES OF NAVIGATORS

Bennett encouraged Emma De Long not to worry about "the silly prophesies" of his rival papers. He sent her a telegram to say that he was "perfectly confident of absolute safety of ship and crew and consider the fact of their not being heard from is a good sign of success."

Bennett's encouragement didn't stop Emma from worrying. "The *Herald*'s competitors had not been slow to take the opportunity to state their pessimistic views," she wrote. "It was too good a chance to miss."

Emma wrote lengthy "letters to nowhere" to her husband. She sent them north on ships with the hope they'd meet up with the *Jeannette*. One letter ran fifty-three pages. She made three copies and sent them on three different ships. "I am well but I suffer from nervousness at times, although I always control it," she wrote in one letter. "I have made it a point not to be affected by any newspaper reports I read, as I reason they know no more about your whereabouts than I do, and therefore I will hope for the best. If I did pay any attention to the reports I could not live, for one day they prophesy the complete loss of the *Jeannette* and the next her complete safety."

John Danenhower's father, a prominent politician and editor, was confident that the officers and crew of the *Jeannette* were safe. He boasted to the *Chicago Tribune* that his son and his brave companions were fully prepared for whatever they might encounter. "They did not go on a summer excursion, but sailed with a determination of reaching a higher degree of latitude than any of their predecessors," he said.

"I have no doubt she reached her destination and quartered for the winter where her officers expected. . . . I confidently expect her safe return next fall."

George W. De Long Journal

MARCH 1, MONDAY

Danenhower had the sixth operation on his eye today. . . . The knife and probe are regular things in his case now, and come at regularly shortening intervals. There is no sign of improvement. Day after day it is the same old story. He bears his confinement and the pain of the operations heroically, and his general health and spirits keep up well. But he will never be of any use to the expedition.

APRIL 6TH, TUESDAY

Although the sun is below the horizon for about eight hours, we have daylight the whole twenty-four hours. That is to say I consider enough daylight existing at midnight to navigate the ship were there open water to make it possible.

APRIL 18TH, SUNDAY

From aloft the view is far less discouraging than it was a month ago. Then the ice-field was all broken up by confused masses and heaps of shattered floes, the result of the winter's conflicts. Under such circumstances I fear five miles a day would have been an impossibility with loaded sledges.

Now these masses are greatly reduced, and though rough and hummocky they are not impossible to pass; I think a mile an hour might be made without great difficulty. Then if we had been forced to abandon our ship by her being destroyed we could have reached the Siberian settlements only by a miracle; now, if our ship by some accident is taken from us, our chances of reaching Siberia, or open water, are greatly in our favor.

CHAPTER 9

First Mates

S mike, Snoozer, Bismarck, Plug Ugly. Life on a frozen ship wasn't easy for men or dogs, but the forty dogs always made the best of it. "They seem perfectly oblivious to all surroundings, utterly indifferent whether the sun shines or does not shine, so long as they are fed," De Long wrote. "From the liberal diet of bear meat and seals' entrails they have remained as fat as dumplings."

The men, of course, had their favorites. The dog named Paddy received special treatment on St. Patrick's Day. He wore a green ribbon and earned an unusually warm bed alongside an engine.

But the dogs weren't pets. They worked hard, and their lives sometimes took a brutal turn.

Bingo died first. He'd been part of a team that dragged a sled over the ice while the men searched for a walrus they'd killed the day before. Somehow, Bingo slipped out of his harness and ran off, "much to the disgust of the other dogs," De Long wrote, "who attempted to chase him. Alexey in his peculiar language remarked, 'Bom bye, other dogs him plenty whip' (for his desertion)."

Alexey was right. After Bingo returned to the ship, the other dogs attacked and killed him.

The rowdy dogs were often fighting.

The dogs scavenged the ice for cast-off cans and other scraps.

It was a sad moment, but there wasn't much room for sentimentality. A dead animal could supply nourishment and clothing. "We skinned him to have his coat for future wearing apparel, and his carcass lies frozen on the deckhouse roof for possible food for his murderers," De Long wrote.

Hard-Working Jack perished, too. Like most of the dogs, he spent time scavenging for bones and other castoffs on the ice. His "premature demise" was caused by eating mutton bones, two sharp pieces of a tin can, a bit of cloth, and a hunk of rope.

But the most damage occurred when a large pack of dogs went after a relatively small bear. The bruin "came up from astern . . . and when about five hundred yards distant was sighted by the dogs, about twenty of whom made for him and brought him to," De Long wrote. The bear climbed a hummock and the dogs charged him, while William Nindemann and another crewman raced over with rifles.

The bear fought desperately, flinging the dogs left and

right. Charles Chipp, watching the battle from the deck, reported that "when the dogs charged the fur would fly, and then a dog would be sent through the air, torn and repulsed."

Nindemann finally got off a shot, which passed through the bear, glanced off a bone, and killed Plug Ugly.

"When injuries came to be examined, we found it a very costly bit of bear," De Long wrote. Plug Ugly was dead; Prince, Wolf, and Snoozer were bleeding badly; and others had been gashed by the bear's claws and teeth.

The bear, which turned out to be a female, weighed 374 pounds. "Ordinarily they do not fight much, generally jumping around and around to keep face to the dogs," De Long wrote. But that bear was ready for war.

Poor Plug Ugly lost his life to a bear.

George W. De Long Journal

APRIL 30, FRIDAY

Chipp observed a flock of about twenty ducks (eiders) flying high and steering west. No doubt they were bound for some land in that direction, but though we strained our eyes and glasses as the sun got around there we could see none of it.

MAY 7, FRIDAY

Each day finds our coal pile diminishing, and no sign yet

of weather which would make it safe to stop our fires on the berth-deck and in the cabin. A temperature of 32 would be as acceptable as possible, although it is the freezing point of fresh water. This day commences with a temperature of minus 3.7. . . . The weather is gloomy, depressing, and disagreeable.

JUNE 3D, THURSDAY

As to there being any warm current reaching to a high latitude, I very much doubt. We have found none. . . . I pronounce a thermometric gate-way to the Pole a delusion and a snare. Of course if any warm current came through Behring Strait it would be the Kuro Siwo, and our sea temperatures indicated no such fact.

JULY 10TH, SATURDAY

A day of almost steady rain and fog, and to my sensation, more disagreeable in temperature than the coldest weather of winter. The thermometer ranged between 30 and 34.5, but the dampness and moisture seemed to pierce to the bone and marrow.

CHAPTER 10

A Menacing Encounter

De Long stepped into a dinghy and shoved off into the narrow stream. He blew out his breath in a cold mist, rowing slowly to avoid crashing into the channel's icy walls. Though reaching the open ocean was out of the question, the captain enjoyed exploring the small streams that opened up in the ice. Most summer afternoons, he set out alone in the dinghy, searching for an escape route for the *Jeannette*.

He knew that the channels would soon freeze over, forcing him and his crew to spend a second winter in the ice pack. That was disappointing but not unexpected. Still, it had been more than a year since he'd seen his wife and daughter. Nearly a year had gone by since he'd stood on land.

It was a Sunday. August 22, 1880. De Long's thirty-sixth birthday.

The stream was so narrow that in some spots he could use only a single oar. Deliberately he poked along through the "winding and intricate" channel, searching for cracks and openings, "watching the wasting of the ice, and making out in my own mind where a break may occur by connecting the several holes wasted clear through to the deep water."

De Long was bewildered by the massive expanse of ice, which seemed more permanent than anyone had believed. "Is this always a dead sea?" he wondered. "Does the ice ever find an outlet?" He'd witnessed nine months of ice growth in the long Arctic winter, and the modest melting during this short hint of summer "by no means equals the growth in nine months." If more ice grew every year than could melt, "it would require but a few years to make this a solid mass, and so take up this Arctic Ocean entirely." Forget about a warm polar sea.

De Long rowed for about a mile, but because of all the twists and turns in the mazelike channel, he was never more than five hundred yards from the *Jeannette*. He found the solitude a welcome break from the demands of captaining the crew.

He gazed ahead at the seemingly unending ice. How far did it stretch? "It is hard to believe that an impenetrable barrier of ice exists clear up to the Pole," he wrote, "and yet as far as we have gone we have not seen one speck of land north of Herald Island."

The dinghy entered a long, thin opening, "which obliged me to scull, and facing aft, to use both hands." Something caused De Long to look back over his shoulder, "and to my astonishment found my eyes resting on a bear not a hundred feet off, and who, judging by his looks, was quite as astonished as I was."

De Long looked for a way to escape, but the prospects were bleak. There was no water between him and the bear, and the piles of ice would make it impossible for him to

De Long was shocked when he came face-to-face with a polar bear.

outrun the animal. "I was jammed in a narrow lead and he stood looking at me."

Then the bear stepped toward him.

"On board ship there!" De Long yelled. "A bear! a bear!"

No one answered.

The bear had advanced to within fifty feet—"so close that I could see distinctly where the short hair ended at the edge of his beautiful black nose. Hearing my shout he stopped, and looked at me wonderingly. I again shouted, 'On board ship there!' and somebody answered, 'Halloa.' Mentally calculating my chances I again yelled, 'A bear! a bear!'"

De Long lifted an oar, ready to fight the bear if it attacked. "He stood still, however, and looked as if he could not quite make me out."

The bear hesitated. The barking of a pack of dogs—turned loose from the ship and answering De Long's call—caught the bear's attention. "He gazed at them until, judging they meant him no good, he turned and ran, so fast that before the men and dogs could get on his trail he was out of range."

De Long recorded the event in his journal that evening: "Lesson for me: 'Never go away from the ship without a rifle.'"

Within a week of De Long's encounter with the bear, any lingering hope of a warm summer had faded away. De Long resigned himself to a second winter in the ice, but "Shall we be any more successful when it has passed?" Careful measurements showed that the *Jeannette* had drifted about

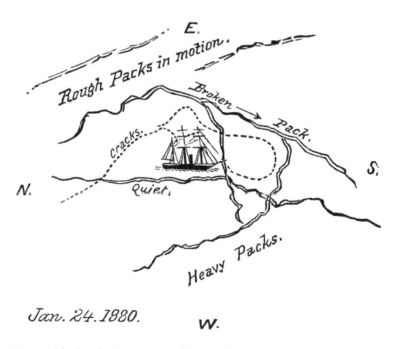

Jan. 24. 1880.

Newcomb's sketch shows many of the cracks that formed streams in the ice pack.

140 miles north from the point where it first had been locked in nearly a year before. De Long gloomily speculated that with a similar drift through the next year, "we shall then be 800 miles from the Pole, and 500 miles from a Siberian settlement, with a disabled ship, no fuel, and perhaps as immovably jammed as now."

And though the food and fuel would never last, De Long imagined the possibilities of a deserted ship continuing in a never-ending northward spiral. "In six additional years we should reach the Pole. But what is the use of figuring it up—a man might as well attempt to demonstrate by mathematical calculation the day of his death. Let us deal with the present."

George W. De Long Journal

SEPTEMBER 2D, THURSDAY

A cheerless and gloomy day. The usual fog in the fore-noon, and in the afternoon until midnight an almost steady fall of very light snow. In one day we seem to have jumped into winter.

SEPTEMBER 5TH, SUNDAY

One year in the ice! and we are only one hundred and fifty miles to the northward and westward of where we entered it. . . . Anxiety, disappointment, difficulties, troubles, are all so inseparably mixed that I am unable to select any one for a beginning.

OCTOBER 5TH, TUESDAY

At six A. M. Chipp heard a grinding of ice to the eastward, and I suppose we shall have the satisfaction now of waiting for the repetition of the anxious times of last winter, not knowing how soon we may have pandemonium around us. In order to provide for any emergencies we can do nothing more than getting provisions on deck, convenient for heaving on the ice, and we therefore devote the day to this occupation.

RAYMOND NEWCOMB:

The snow would give a metallic ring at each footfall loud enough to interfere with ordinary conversation. Standing near some of these conflicts between grinding floes one first would realize the pressure by the humming, buzzing sound; then a pulsation is felt . . . right under foot, with a report like a big gun. . . . It upheaves you, lifts you with it and you must step back to a safer place. I have often taken these rides. There is a wonderful fascination about it.

CHAPTER 11

---◆◇◆---

"Awful Beauty"

D e Long had been lying in his bunk for two hours, tossing and turning and thinking. After more than a year of the same routine and the same food, his lack of physical work had affected his sleep. Most nights he lay awake until after 3 a.m., finally catching a few hours of sleep before waking "dull and heavy, having no feeling of rest obtained."

Staring at the ceiling, De Long worried about the health of his men, whom the doctor had determined had "a general want of tone and less vigor than last year. As this is exactly what would result from our life of enforced monotony and prolonged absence from land, there is no surprise to be manifested."

On this night, he returned to his usual worry that the expedition had accomplished little. By now he'd expected to have discovered new islands, explored regions where no human had ever set foot, and even found a route to the North Pole. Instead he was stuck fast in the ice for a second winter.

A more immediate concern was the shrinking piles of coal on board the *Jeannette*, and the lesser quality of what remained. "I am very much afraid that our expenditure of fuel this winter will be much greater than last winter," he wrote. "We are coming to much fine dusty stuff, a Nanaimo coal, which burns like powder, and requires a large quantity to generate heat. Last winter we had much anthracite coal in our daily issue, and that lasted longer and did better work."

The ice pack began to grind again, raising concerns that the ship might not withstand another winter in the pack.

In the dark night, De Long lay still and planned for the inevitable abandoning of the ship, going over lists of provisions in his head and figuring out how the crew could haul the supplies over the piled-up ice.

"Pemmican [a chewy mixture of dried beef, fat, and dried berries], bread, tea, sugar, cooking-stoves, alcohol, tents, and sleeping-bags are all that we can hope to be able to drag should we have to leave the ship, adding, of course, our knapsacks, medical stores, instruments, arms and ammunition, and our records," he wrote. "If we can get over the two hundred and fifty and odd miles between us and Siberia with this load we shall do well."

Shaking off his covers, De Long headed up to the deck. The temperature was well below zero, but he wasn't bothered by the cold. The scene that greeted him looked beautiful beyond words, and he allowed himself a moment of satisfaction. He and his crew were farther north than anyone had ever gone. That alone was meaningful. Few people would ever take in a view like this.

Though the captain usually resisted writing anything "poetical," on this night—October 16, 1880—he succeeded in capturing the breathtaking glory of the Arctic:

Imagine a moon nearly full, a cloudless sky, brilliant stars, a pure white waste of snow-covered ice, which seems firm and crisp under your feet, a ship standing out in bold relief, every rope and thread plainly visible and enormously enlarged by accumulations of fluffy and down-like frost feathers; and you have a crude picture of the scene. But to fill in and properly understand the situation, one must experience the majestic and awful silence which generally prevails on these occasions, and causes one to feel how trifling and insignificant he is in comparison with such grand works in nature. The brightness is wonderful. The reflection of moonlight from bright ice-spots makes brilliant effects, and should a stray piece of tin be near you it seems to have the light of a dazzling gem. A window in the deck-house looks like a calcium light when the moonlight strikes it at the proper angle, and makes the feeble light from an oil lamp within seem ridiculous when the angle is changed. Standing one hundred yards away from the ship, one has a scene of the grandest, wildest, and most awful beauty.

Back home, assurances continued that the *Jeannette* expedition was thriving, even though there was no evidence that this was true. In December of 1880, the California Academy of Sciences reported that "we may feel assured that the *Jeannette* is safe and sound, and her Polar voyage of scientific exploration is proceeding favorably according to the plan of its enterprising and generous patron, and it is fair to presume that she passed northward along the unknown coast of Wrangel Land beyond immediate communication, just as all on board fully hoped and intended."

George W. De Long Journal

CHRISTMAS, DECEMBER 25TH, SATURDAY

The day was made as acceptable as possible fore and aft, by the providing of a good dinner from our resources. And I think we may refer to our bills of fare with pardonable pride. Our mince pies were a work of art; though they were made from pemmican and flavored by a bottle of brandy, they were as delicate to the taste as if compounded from beef fresh from the market.

Christmas Dinner, 1880

CABIN.	BERTH DECK.
The usual Saturday soup.	*Soup.*
Roast Seal, Apple Jelly.	*Roast Seal, Apple Jelly.*
Tongue.	*Bacon (broiled).*
Macaroni.	*Macaroni.*
Tomatoes.	*Tomatoes.*
Mince Pies.	*Mince Pies.*
Plum Pudding.	*Figs.*
Figs.	*Raisins.*
Raisins.	*Dates.*
Dates.	*Nuts.*
Nuts.	*Candy.*
Candy.	*Chocolate or Coffee.*
Chocolate and Coffee.	

JANUARY 1ST, 1881, SATURDAY

Melville and Dunbar sat up with me to see the old year out and the new year in. At midnight, when the men had finished a verse and chorus from "Marching through Georgia," eight bells were struck for the old year, three cheers were given for the ship, eight bells more were struck for the new year, and 1881 was thus officially inaugurated in the United States Arctic Steamer Jeannette.

JANUARY 19TH, WEDNESDAY

One year ago to-day we had our serious trouble with the ice and received our injuries. Since that time the water has steadily come into the ship, and has been as steadily pumped out.

FEBRUARY 5TH, SATURDAY

This year we have not been disturbed at all. The doctor puts it very well when he says, "Last winter I went to bed expecting to be turned out, and was surprised that I was not; but this winter I go to bed expecting not to be turned out, and would be very much surprised if I were."

FEBRUARY 24TH, THURSDAY

Another instance of extraordinary change of temperature in twenty-four hours. Yesterday we had minus 42.5°, and to-day we get minus 1°! Who wants more than that to make him happy?

GEORGE W. MELVILLE:

This was our second winter in the ice; and in the history of all previous expeditions, scurvy, the bane of the Arctic voyager, had made its dread appearance long ere such an interval had elapsed. Why were we exempt? . . . Like vegetables grown in the dark, we were bleached to an unnatural pallor; and as spring approached all exhibited signs of debility. Sleep was fortunately peaceful and undisturbed, by reason of the floe's solidity; but certain members of the mess were attacked with fits of indigestion; Mr. Dunbar [the ice pilot] became very ill; and an ugly ulcer appeared on [Alexey's] leg accompanied by other symptoms which raised suspicions of the presence of scurvy.

George W. De Long Journal

MARCH 1ST, TUESDAY

The medical examination being concluded to-day, the doctor handed in his report. It is, on the whole, satisfactory. Six are in good condition, and two (Mr. Danenhower and Mr. Dunbar) fair. All hands forward are in good condition except Alexey, and his condition is fair. The doctor reports that a want of tone prevails; that is, we are not as vigorous and could not stand exposure and prolonged muscular exertion as we might have done when we first reached the ice.

MAY 16TH, MONDAY

LAND! There is something then besides ice in the world. . . . Of course I dropped my books and ran up to the fore yard, and there, sure enough, I saw a small island one half point forward of our starboard beam, the first land that has greeted our eyes since March 24, 1880, nearly fourteen months ago. And our voyage, thank God, is not a perfect blank, for here we have discovered something, however small it may be. . . . What this poor desolate island, standing among icy wastes, may have to do in the economy of nature I do not know, or in fact care. It is solid land, whether of volcanic origin or otherwise, and will stand still long enough to let a man realize where he is. Moreover, this must be the spot to which the ducks and geese have been steadily flying, and if we can get some of them for a change to our canned meats, what a treat! And then bears must swarm on our island! In fine, this island is to us our all in all. We gaze at it, we criticise it, we guess at its distance, we wish for a favoring gale to drive us towards it. . . . Fourteen months without anything to look at but ice and sky, and twenty months drifting in the pack, will make a little mass of volcanic rock like our island as pleasing to the eye as an oasis in the desert.

CHAPTER 12

Grinding, Crashing, and Rolling

George Melville stared at the treacherous, broken ice pack, "thrown into chaotic masses in all directions and in all forms imaginable. Great anxiety was now felt for the safety of the ship, as the whole ice-field, pack and floe, seemed in rapid motion."

The *Jeannette* had drifted past the island seen a few days earlier, but ice pilot William Dunbar spotted another one from

Melville made this sketch of Jeannette Island as the ship drifted past it.

the crow's nest that might be reachable. It was smaller and less mountainous than the first, which De Long had dubbed Jeannette Island. This new one on the horizon would be named Henrietta Island, for James Gordon Bennett Jr.'s mother.

Petermann's map didn't show any islands within a hundred miles of the area. But that shouldn't have been a surprise. De Long had found that Petermann was wrong about many things: Wrangel Land didn't extend very far north and certainly didn't come close to Greenland; the Kuro Siwo current ran out of steam well before reaching the polar region; and there were virtually no sources of drinkable water on the ice.

De Long asked Melville if he would lead an expedition to the smaller island. Most of the crewmen were doubtful that such a trek would succeed, but "there was no scarcity of volunteers."

Melville never shied away from a challenge. On June 1, he and Dunbar, carpenter William Nindemann, and crewmen Hans Ericksen, James Bartlett, and Walter Sharvell set out with fifteen dogs. The dogs pulled a sled and the men dragged a dinghy. The island appeared to be about fifteen to twenty miles away.

They immediately ran into trouble. After traveling just five hundred yards, they reached an opening in the ice and had to ferry across the water in the dinghy. But the dogs balked at the water, and several ran back to the ship.

"The thermometers registered many degrees below freezing point; the boat was covered with ice, our clothes were wet, and our hands frost-bitten," Melville wrote. But there was no turning back. Men who'd stayed behind on the

Jeannette caught the dogs and returned them to Melville. The dogs were dragged through the water and pulled across. "It was cruel, I know, but there was no alternative," Melville wrote. Once the dogs had crossed and were hitched to the sled, "the poor shivering brutes were soon warming themselves in the hard work ahead of them."

The men were working hard, too. They each wore "ruy ruddies," canvas harnesses that fastened to their waists so they could help pull the sled. They toiled for twelve hours— "making roads, filling up chasms with 'hummocky bits,' and jumping the team across them"—before pitching the tent and collapsing into sleep.

Melville estimated that they'd covered four miles "and made no appreciable gain on the island."

After a breakfast of pigs' feet and mutton broth, they struggled off again. "The condition of the ice, grinding, crashing, and telescoping, sometimes pitching and rolling in such a manner as to render foothold impossible, made our enterprise a particularly perilous one," Melville wrote.

After three exhausting days, "the island at length loomed up before us in all its cloud-crowned majesty." Black, serrated rocks rose straight up from the coast. Red streaks of iron added to the starkness of the cliffs, which rose four hundred feet. Snow and ice capped the higher peaks beyond.

But between Melville and the island raged an overwhelming cauldron: "great bodies of ice were incessantly fleeing, it seemed, from the mad pursuit of those behind; now hurling themselves on top, and now borne down and buried by others.

And it was through this chaos of ice that we must force our way to the island."

Impossible as it seemed, Melville decided to leave the dinghy and most of the supplies to make "a dash for the land across the broken ice, jumping from bit to bit." He stashed the equipment and food on a high hummock (a ridge of ice), lashing a small black flag to an oar and standing it in the ice as a marker.

By then, Dunbar was suffering from severe snow blindness. He begged to be left behind to wait, but Melville said no. The men splashed through the ice and slush, dragging Dunbar on the sled.

"We waded and struggled through the posh and water, the sled wholly immersed, with Mr. Dunbar still clinging to the crossbars and Ericksen performing herculean feats of strength," Melville wrote. "More than once, when the sled stuck fast, did he place his brawny shoulders under the boot and lift it bodily out. Indeed, we all toiled so hard that when the ridge at the edge of the ice-foot was reached, we were barely able to crawl over it and drag Dunbar from the sea like some great seal."

As a commissioned officer, Melville was the first to set foot on the island. He planted a flag and claimed the island as a territory of the United States.

Powerful Hans Ericksen was suddenly incapacitated, too. He experienced snow blindness and a bout of painful stomach cramps. Nindemann had severe cramps as well.

The cramping mystified Melville. What he couldn't have known was that the crew back on the *Jeannette* was suffering from it, too.

George W. De Long Journal

JUNE 1ST, WEDNESDAY

What next? The doctor informs me this morning that he is of opinion that several of our party under his treatment are suffering from lead poisoning. Newcomb is quite under the weather with severe colic [stomach pains], and Kuehne is about the same.

JUNE 2D, THURSDAY

Our lead invalids are responding to treatment, the steward [Charles Tong Sing] more slowly than the rest, as his attack was the most severe.

JUNE 3D, FRIDAY

Nothing yet to be seen of Melville and his party. Taking all things into consideration, I do not expect him before to-morrow night or Sunday morning; but though neither of these times are here yet, I cannot help the constant uneasiness which I experience.

CHAPTER 13

━━▷◦◁━━

Poisoned!

D r. Ambler suspected that the ship's water had been tainted with lead, since the distiller's joints were sealed with the metal. But a test showed that it wasn't the water. A few grains of shot turned up in some of the birds they were eating, and that might have been another source of lead. But the true cause remained a mystery until someone bit into a pellet of solder while eating his favorite dish. "Who shot the tomatoes?" he joked.

It was the other way around. The tomatoes had been targeting the men for months. The cans were sealed with lead solder, and the acid of the contents (which was particularly high in tomatoes) had leached the lead from the sealant. The men had been eating canned tomatoes four times a week for nearly two years, so De Long suspected that the

Dr. James Ambler

⊰ 91 ⊱

leaching had built up over time, making the tomatoes more toxic now than before.

After enduring so many incredible hardships, the men were in danger of dying from canned tomatoes! "What use is it to secure exemption from scurvy for two years if disabling lead poison finishes you in the third year?" De Long asked.

Back on Henrietta Island, Melville made sketches of the headlands, mountain range, and hummocks. The men shot a few seabirds—black-and-white guillemots—"which nestled among the rocks in great numbers. These were the only birds seen; indeed, we saw no other living thing."

Melville climbed a hill and built a rock cairn. In the pile, he placed a copper cylinder containing a note from De Long describing the *Jeannette*'s journey so far. He also left a zinc case holding several old copies of Bennett's *New York Herald*.

The men started back for the ship, but the ice had grown even more treacherous. Dunbar's eyes had not improved, so the men and dogs again pulled him on the sled. Crossing a floe, the ice began to wobble. The men jumped aside, but the dogs slipped into the water "and dragged the sled, with Mr. Dunbar sprawled out on top, bodily through the slush and water to the firm ice, while we roared with laughter," Melville wrote.

Melville worried that they might not find the *Jeannette*. Because of fog and the high hummocks, they couldn't see the ship or their stash of provisions, and didn't see any of their previous tracks in the snow. They were out of food.

Finally, the weather cleared slightly and Ericksen saw the oar and the flag. "From this time on, . . . the weather was miserable," Melville said. Navigating by compass, "we marched forward in the face of a cruel snow and wind storm, constantly impeded by open lanes and leads of water."

They pitched the tent to rest for the evening, freezing and worried. Dunbar winced with pain from his eye condition. Ericksen's skin was severely chafed from the cold wind and his wet clothing. Nindemann's stomach cramps worsened. "Poor Nindemann, drawn and doubled up, was enduring the agonies of the lost," Melville noted.

Melville took out the small medicine box. A dose of capsicum might relieve Nindemann's pain, and some "sweet-oil" could relieve Ericksen's skin problem. But Melville's fingers were too cold and sore to open the bottles, so he handed them to Ericksen to remove the corks.

"He drew them with a reckless abandon," Melville recalled, "spilling the tincture of capsicum (cayenne pepper raised to the nth power) over his cracked and blistered hands. Then, losing his head completely, he applied the sweet-oil by means of his fiery fingers to the afflicted portions of his body."

The pepper stung terribly. Ericksen "rolled and squirmed about in the snow like an eel." Then he tore off his clothes to ease the burning even more.

"Nindemann laughed his cramps away," Melville wrote, "and Dunbar found time between his groans to shout out, — 'Ericksen, are you hot enough to make the snow hiss?'"

One more day of struggle brought the men to the ship. On board, De Long heard a shot as the men announced their approach. In his excitement, De Long rushed up to the bridge to see them, and "crash! I got a terrible blow on the head" as a wing of the windmill smashed into him. "Stunned and confused I crawled back, while the blood sprinkled on the ladder and quarter deck." Dr. Ambler stitched up the four-inch gash, "and then I resumed my scrutiny of the returning party."

De Long was relieved to have the men back. His eyes sparkled as he greeted Melville: "Well done, old fellow."

De Long could not have been prouder that the risky expedition had paid off. "Thank God, we have at least landed upon a newly discovered part of this earth," he recorded, "and a perilous journey has been accomplished without disaster."

GEORGE W. MELVILLE:

We were all persuaded that the chances of the ship holding together, in the present state of the ice, were not one in a thousand. Yet she might, but what then? This was the supreme question which constantly presented itself to the minds of all: whether it would not be wiser to abandon the ship at once, and make for the nearest land (New Siberian Islands), instead of tarrying for the fall travel. De Long naturally wished to stay by the ship until the end, or so long as the provisions lasted, proposing that we remain until they had dwindled down to an allowance of ninety days for our retreat.

George W. De Long Journal

JUNE 6TH, MONDAY

Lanes and openings were forming and closing during all the forenoon, and every once in a while the sudden rearing up of some ridge of broken floe pieces, twenty and thirty feet high, showed where a lane had closed, or the sudden tumbling of a mound showed where a lane was opening. . . . Had our floe broken up and hurled us adrift we should have had the liveliest time in our cruise, for to have escaped destruction would have been a miracle, and to have got anything or any person out of the ship in case of accident an impossibility.

JUNE 8TH, WEDNESDAY

We are leaving Henrietta Island rapidly to the eastward of us, and before many days it may be lost to view. Inasmuch as we have passed it already, one might call it a thing of the past. (I am afraid that is a poor joke, but since the windmill struck me I can do no better.)

JUNE 11TH, SATURDAY, [1881]

At four P. M. the ice came down in great force all along the port side, jamming the ship hard against the ice on the starboard side of her, and causing her to heel 16° to starboard. From the snapping and cracking of the bunker sides and starting in of the starboard ceiling, as well as the opening of the seams in the ceiling to the width of one and one fourth inches, it was feared that the ship was about to be seriously endangered.

CHAPTER 14

Catastrophe

At first, Melville thought someone had fired a gun, but the *crack* was the violent splitting of the ice that held the *Jeannette*. He and the rest of the crew raced to the deck as the ship wobbled and creaked.

Dogs barked from a wide chunk of ice that had broken off and floated one hundred yards away. The ship tilted sharply. Its masts and smokestacks buck-led, and sections caved

The men pitched tents and gathered provisions as the *Jeannette* slowly sank.

in. Newcomb watched as the gang ladders leading to the bridge "jumped from their chucks, and danced on the deck like drumsticks on the head of a drum."

De Long stood on the ice with his friend William Dunbar. They both knew that the *Jeannette* was a goner. "Well, what do you think of it?" De Long asked anyway.

"She will either be under the floe or on top of it before to-morrow night," Dunbar replied.

The *Jeannette* was sinking. Everyone expected it; everyone was prepared; but no one could possibly know what would happen next. The men went to work removing food and equipment from the ship.

"Preparations had been made for such a catastrophe ever since we entered the ice," Melville explained. "Every officer and man had his appointed duty to perform, and hence there was neither noise nor confusion."

The evacuation went smoothly, even though the ship leaned so far over that the men found it impossible to stand without holding on to something.

Incredibly, they were in good spirits. "In fact," Melville recalled, "as the men passed the stuff over the side, they were singing merchant-ship songs."

Only executive officer Chipp, suffering from chills and a fever, needed help to gather his clothing and other materials. Though Lieutenant Danenhower remained on the sick list, he gathered the charts and instruments. But as he started down the ladder to the wardroom, he stepped into icy water. The ship was flooding rapidly. A crewman dived beneath the water to salvage two cases of ammunition—critical for the long trek ahead of them. Then he went under again, this time grabbing a barrel of lime juice.

With the hold full of water, De Long ordered everyone off. He waved his Navy cap and called, "Good by, old ship!"

Three smaller boats had been lowered to the ice: two cutters and a whaleboat. They sat beside a large trove of food and equipment, as well as the ship's heavy logbooks.

The men pitched their tents and waited. De Long took inventory of the provisions on the ice—far more than the crew could hope to carry. He recorded nearly five thousand pounds of pemmican, more than half a ton of hard bread, nine hundred pounds of canned meat and soup, and ample amounts of sugar, tea, and coffee.

De Long noted that "beside the contents of the packed knapsacks, and the clothing in wear, we find we have the following:

28 over-shirts (woolen),
24 drawers,

27 under-shirts (woolen),
24 sack-coats,
8 overcoats,
20 trousers (cloth),
8 fur blankets,
18 woolen blankets,
13 skin parkies,—
and they were divided among all hands as required, much
of it being in excess."

As the men slept in their tents nearby, the ship slowly sank, taking Newcomb's stuffed birds, the toxic tomatoes, Melville's photographs, and hundreds of other items with it. By 4 a.m. on June 12, only the two crewmen who were assigned to keep watch remained awake to see her go under. "There she goes; hurry up and have a look, the last sight you will have of the old *Jeannette*," one shouted.

The ship went down in about 38 fathoms of water (228 feet).

By morning, "everybody seems bright and cheerful, with plenty to eat and plenty of clothes," De Long wrote.

De Long and some others visited the site of the wreck. They found one chair on the ice, some oars, and broken planks.

The captain was in no hurry to begin the grueling trek toward Siberia. The men on the sick list, particularly Chipp, Danenhower, and Alexey, were improving, and a few more days of recuperation would "tend to their advantage." He planned to haul enough provisions for eighty days of travel.

The men would be cold, wet, hungry, and exhausted every second, but the crew of "honest Jacks" was very much alive and determined.

In this romanticized painting, De Long tips his cap to the sinking *Jeannette*. Depicted to De Long's left are Melville, Danenhower, and Alexey.

"And here we were, cast out upon the ice five hundred miles from the mouth of the Lena River, our nearest hope of succor; with a sick list, and a limited supply of food," Melville wrote. "Yet, although the seriousness of our situation was appreciated by all, none were despondent, many merry, and shortly after the boatswain 'piped down,' the whole camp was lost in slumber.

"And thankful were we to make our beds on snow instead of beneath the sea, where honest Jack so often finds his endless rest."

CHAPTER 15

———◆———

"Superhuman Exertions"

Because there had been no word from the *Jeannette* for nearly two years, several expeditions were sent to look for it. While the *Jeannette* was sinking, the U.S.R.C. *Thomas Corwin* searched the Siberian coast, hundreds of miles away. That same ship had carried Alexey and Edward Nelson into the Yukon in 1879. Nelson was on board again, along with naturalist John Muir (who later in life helped create the U.S. National Park Service). Muir had little interest in the rescue mission; he'd signed up so he could study Arctic glaciers. "The clouds lifted from the mountains, showing their bases and slopes up to a thousand feet; summits capped," he wrote from the deck on June 4.

"Of course, if De Long is found we will return at once," Muir noted as the *Corwin* chugged north. But the ship returned home with no news of the *Jeannette*. Later that summer, the secretary of the Navy sent the U.S.S. *Rodgers* on a search as far as the ice pack, and Bennett funded a trip to the North Atlantic, in case the *Jeannette* had reached Greenland.

Dragging the boats and sleds over the ice took incredible effort.

By then, the *Jeannette* rested at the bottom of the sea. The crew and captain were still on the ice. Survival was their only goal now, and they prepared to begin a do-or-die trek to Siberia. De Long wrote a letter to document the situation. He explained when and where the ship had sunk and that the crew was about to head for the New Siberian Islands with eighty days' worth of provisions.

De Long sewed up his letter in a piece of black rubber and put it in an empty cask. Then he left it on the ice in the hope that it "may get somewhere." A large pile of clothing and food was also left behind, including Louis Noros's sealskin pants.

De Long was as well prepared as ever. He issued precise orders for the distribution of food and equipment in each of the sleds and the boats; for the daily schedule of travel, meals, breaks, and sleep; and for what each man would wear. "The clothing allowance for each officer and man will be limited to what he actually wears and the contents of his packed knapsack. Each may dress in skins or not as he pleases at the start, but having made his choice, he must be ready to abide by it. Extra outside clothing of any kind (except moccasins) cannot be taken, so much was left behind. The contents of the packed knapsacks are to be as follows:

2 pairs blanket nips, or duffle nips,
2 pairs stockings,
1 pair moccasins,
1 cap,
2 pairs mittens,
1 undershirt,
1 pair drawers,
1 skull-cap,
1 comforter,
1 pair snow spectacles,
1 plug tobacco,
1 pipe,
20 rounds ammunition,
24 wind matches.
Soap, towels, thread and needles at discretion."

The rations would be spare, and there'd be no variety unless the men shot some seals or bears along the way.

Breakfast.	*Dinner.*	*Supper.*
4 oz. pemmican,	*8 oz. pemmican,*	*4 oz. pemmican,*
1 oz. ham,	*1 oz. Liebig,*	*1 oz. tongue,*
3 pieces bread,	*½ oz. tea,*	*½ oz. tea,*
2 oz. coffee,	*⅔ oz. sugar.*	*⅔ oz. sugar,*
⅔ oz. sugar.		*1 oz. lime juice,*
		¼ lb. bread.

De Long set an ambitious routine, with a plan to travel at night. There would be less glare from the sun then, and the ice that melted during the day would freeze solid in the colder night air, making for smoother travel.

Call all hands	*4.30 P. M.*
Breakfast	*5.00*
Break camp	*5.40*
Under way	*6.00*
Halt	*11.30*
Dinner	*Midnight*
Pack up	*12.40 A. M.*
Under way	*1.00*
Halt, pitch camp	*6.00*
Lime juice	*6.00*
Supper	*6.30*
Set watch, pipe down, turn in	*7.00*

De Long divided the men into several work crews. He hoped that each crew could move a boat or a sled independently, but that theory was immediately shot to pieces. Advancing the heavy gear over the broken ice took "superhuman exertions," and most of the available crew was needed to move each boat or sled. (The men on the sick list did not work. Chipp, in fact, was so weak from lead poisoning that he had to be pulled in a sled. The others were able to walk.)

"Twenty-eight men and twenty-three dogs laying back with all their strength could only start our sixteen hundred pound sled a few feet each time," De Long wrote in exasperation. The rough, rutted ice made for a nearly impossible path, and before they'd pushed the gear a quarter of a mile, they had broken three sleds.

De Long and Dunbar had laid out the first day's route the

night before, setting up a series of flags as guideposts, and Melville brought a day's provisions forward in advance.

The crew strained to move a boat after strapping on their canvas harnesses. "Aided by these, the men seized the drag-rope, and, surrounding the boat to keep it upright, began hauling it through the deep, soggy snow, which at times reached to our waists," Melville wrote. "Whooping and singing, we at last carried and dragged it as far as the depot of supplies that I had deposited the day before." They thought they were done for the day.

Melville was surprised to learn that there was another flag a half mile ahead. De Long made it clear that they must stay on schedule, so they started again.

The ice began breaking up, causing channels of water. Frantic to get everything to safety, "all hands were placed on one boat or sled at a time, and when the passing floes came together we hurried it over; many of us with a firm grip on the drag-rope dashing into the slush and water 'neck and heels,' to be hauled out by our companions ahead," Melville wrote. Somehow, to the men this all seemed funny! "Amid roars of laughter and good-humored banter, we succeeded late in the afternoon in again bringing all our baggage together."

Even the lightest sleds (which, when loaded, weighed nearly a ton) could be moved only one at a time. Having everyone go back and forth for sleds and boats meant a huge amount of extra work. "To make one mile good in a straight line, we must march thirteen," Melville explained.

With several hundred miles between them and Siberia,

their prospects looked bleak. Eighty days' worth of food wouldn't get them nearly that far.

George W. De Long Journal

JUNE 20TH, MONDAY

At no time of the year is traveling worse than at present. In the winter or spring months it is, of course, cold and comfortless, but it is nevertheless dry. In autumn or late summer it is favorable, because the melted snow has all drained off the hard ice, and the traveling is excellent. But just now the snow is soft enough to sink into, and progress is almost impossible.

JUNE 22D, WEDNESDAY

I hardly had gone one fourth mile when I came to an ice opening, and in spite of my strongest efforts, the dogs scattered across some lumps, capsized the sled, dragged me in, and sent all my mess gear flying, having accomplished which, and reached the other side themselves, they sat down and howled to their hearts' content.

JUNE 24TH, FRIDAY

There is no work in the world harder than this sledging; and with my two line officers [Danenhower and Chipp] constantly on the sick-list, I have much on my hands. In Melville I have a strong support, as well as a substitute for them, and as long as he remains as he is—strong and well—I shall get along all right.

CHAPTER 16

Off Course

De Long could not believe what he saw. He rechecked the position of the sun with the sextant and recalculated the result. It showed that he was at a latitude of 77°46′ N. How could that be? Half a dozen times he tried, and every calculation showed the same thing.

All of their efforts weren't bringing them closer to land. They were drifting farther away!

They'd been pushing south for eight days and covered about sixteen miles. But the drifting ice had taken them three miles to the northwest for every mile they'd walked.

De Long thought about what to do. Telling the crew would devastate their morale. It might even cause a mutiny. So the captain told only Melville and Dr. Ambler, the officers he trusted most.

"If we go on this way we will never get out," De Long wrote. He reset the course to travel southwest instead of due south. Either way, they'd eventually reach open water, but they could not afford to get farther off course or they'd run out of food.

Most days, the crew struggled forward about two miles. During one brutal stretch, it took them twelve hours to move everything just one thousand yards. Men still suffered stomach cramps and weakness from lead poisoning, and the work caused strained muscles, bleeding hands, and exhaustion.

If they could reach the edge of the ice pack, they'd make much faster progress by rowing and sailing in the boats.

At the end of each work day, the men collapsed in the tents. For weeks, Dr. Ambler recorded a steady litany of ailments: stomach cramps and leg cramps, vomiting and diarrhea, swollen glands, faintness, and exhaustion. And especially sore feet. Their moccasins were full of holes, "out of which the water and slush spurted at every step," Melville wrote. "Traveling in summer-time through the water and wet snow, the raw hide softens to the consistency of fresh tripe."

Ambler issued remedies: quinine, cod-liver oil, iodine, liniment. But he was wearing out, too, with stomach troubles and chest pain. "I generally get wet every day and more or less of the skin taken off from some part of me," he wrote.

Ambler checked Danenhower's eye several times a day and saw little improvement. That angered Danenhower, who insisted he was fit and ready to work. He suspected that Ambler and De Long were conspiring to keep him inactive. De Long kept him on the sick list, prohibiting him from doing any labor except walking.

The daily grind continued, and all agreed it was the hardest work they'd ever done. But a cheer arose on July 11. An island!

"The land stood boldly revealed; its blue mountain peaks rising grandly aloft, the ice and water showing plainly below, while a white, dazzling cloud floated dreamily above—in all the most perfect scene of isolated or insular land ever viewed at a distance in the Arctic Ocean," Melville wrote.

Two weeks later, they were still struggling to reach it. The ice kept breaking apart, dumping men and sleds into the water. They were only a half mile from the island, but they couldn't even see it through the fog.

Suddenly, someone shouted, "Look!" As the air cleared, the island's mountains towered directly over them. "It infused new life and vigor into us; and each man straightaway became a Hercules," Melville wrote.

But the ice pack and the men "were sweeping past it like a mill-stream," drifting at three miles an hour.

Several large cakes of ice converged, causing a temporary slowdown. "This was our last chance," De Long knew. "Over two weeks of dragging and working to reach this island seemed about to be thrown away."

Their ice floe spun toward a solid chunk that appeared to connect to the island. If they crashed into it, they might be able to cross the ice bridge to land.

"Now is the time!" De Long shouted as they smacked into it. Two sleds were pushed across, but the third went overboard and so did boatswain Jack Cole. He scrambled up, and somehow the men pulled the sled out of the water.

They were closer to the island, but not on it. The ice-foot they'd reached bordered a fifty-foot gap of churning ice and water, "presenting a simply impassable road for travel with sleds."

The ice-foot itself was solid and not moving. De Long ordered the men to set up camp. They pitched the tents on the ice, then "waded, or jumped, or ferried" through the four-foot-deep water to the island. Most of them hadn't stood on land for two years. They were "sunburned, lean, hungry, and ragged," but also incredibly relieved.

De Long announced that this was a newly discovered island. He claimed it for the United States, naming it Bennett Island. "And never were three more lusty cheers given," he wrote. "With great kindness three were then given for me." De Long named the spot where they'd landed Cape Emma, for his wife.

"This is a magnificent, though desolate, land of rushing torrents, glaciers and huge, impregnable, rocky fastnesses," wrote naturalist Ninky Newcomb, who was thrilled to find more creatures to study. "The birds at this place were in great numbers, the rocks being whitened with their manure. They were coming and going all the time, day and night, cackling, chattering and laughing."

Newcomb even recorded some observations about his own physical reactions to the Arctic. "I notice the cold renders the finger nails brittle."

De Long told the men they'd spend at least a week on the island, repairing the boats and filling up on bird stew. Now that they'd reached open water, they would travel by boat, but all three vessels had been badly damaged by the ice. Carpenter Alfred Sweetman caulked the broken planks and patched them with bits of driftwood.

De Long made the difficult decision to shoot ten dogs, which he said were completely worn out or sick. "The amount of food these ten dogs eat is not compensated for by the work done, and I must think of human life first," he explained.

Twelve dogs remained, including Prince, Smike, and Snoozer.

De Long believed that the island they were on was north

Crewmen struggle ashore at the newly discovered Bennett Island.

of the New Siberian Islands, which did show up on the maps. He planned to navigate through the island chain to the Siberian mainland, expecting to find villages along the Lena River. He relied again on Petermann's words for guidance about the islands, but that amounted to one article—written in German. De Long marked a course on an old, inaccurate chart.

The heavy sleds—so essential for transporting the provisions over the ice—had to be discarded. Trying to tow them would affect the steering of the boats, and lashing them on top would make the boats unstable. Even though they might need the sleds again, they couldn't afford to be slowed down any longer. De Long had them chopped up for firewood.

It was a huge gamble. Winter was setting in, and the men could be trapped by the ice at any time. Without the sleds, moving the loaded boats would be nearly impossible.

Fog, rain, snow, and hail delayed the departure by an extra two days, but August 6 dawned as "the rarest of things in the Arctic—a perfect day. Bright sunshine, almost cloudless, and a burning heat, 27°."

The three boats were loaded "to their utmost capacity."

The first cutter, with De Long in charge, measured 20 feet 4 inches long and 6 feet wide, with six oars. Danenhower described it as "an excellent sea boat."

Danenhower thought the second cutter was quite the opposite— "a very bad sea boat." It was four feet shorter than the first cutter. The ailing Chipp would command the second cutter.

Melville was put in charge of the whaleboat, which angered Danenhower. As the *Jeannette*'s navigator, Danenhower believed he should be in command, despite his eye troubles. That whaleboat was the largest at 25 feet 4 inches and was also considered excellent.

Dr. Ambler insisted that Danenhower shouldn't be in charge of anything. "From his very peculiar mind he has I think gotten the idea in his head that he is being unjustly treated," the doctor wrote. "I do not consider any man who has the affection that he has . . . a fit man to be put in charge of a boat & party of men under any circumstances."

Danenhower argued with De Long about the slight. But De Long angrily told him that he would not risk the safety of other crewmen by giving Danenhower command of the whaleboat. De Long then issued this written order to Melville:

ORDER TO MELVILLE.
U. S. ARCTIC EXPEDITION.
CAPE EMMA, BENNETT ISLAND,
Lat. 76° 38´ N., Long. 148° 20´, E.

August 5th, 1881

P.A. Engineer GEO. W. MELVILLE, U.S. Navy:

SIR, — We shall leave this island to-morrow, steering a course (over ice or through water, as the case may be) south magnetic. In the event of our embarking in our boats at any time after the start, you are hereby ordered to take command of the whaleboat until such time as I relieve you from that duty, or assign you to some other.

Every person under my command at this time, who may be embarked in that boat at any time, is under your charge, and subject to your orders,—and you are to exercise all care and diligence for their preservation and the safety of the boat. You will, under all circumstances, keep close to the boat in which I shall embark, but if, unfortunately, we become separated, you will make the best of your way south until you make the coast of Siberia, and follow it along to the westward as far as the Lena River. This river is the destination of our party, and without delay you will, in case of separation, ascend the Lena to a Russian settlement from which you can communicate, or be forwarded with your party to some place of security and easy access. If the boat in which I am embarked is separated from the two other boats, you will at once place yourself under the orders of Lieutenant C. W. Chipp, and, so long as you remain in company, such orders as he may give you.

Respectfully,

GEORGE W. DE LONG,
Commanding U.S. Arctic Expedition

The boats carried these men
(some men later switched boats):

FIRST CUTTER.	SECOND CUTTER.	WHALEBOAT.
De Long,	Chipp,	Melville,
Ambler,	Dunbar,	Danenhower,
Collins,	Sweetman,	Newcomb,
Nindemann,	Sharvell,	Cole,
Ericksen,	Ericksen,	Bartlett,
Kaack,	Kuehne,	Aneguin,
Boyd,	Starr,	Wilson,
Alexey,	Mansen,	Lauterbach,
Lee,	Warren,	Tong Sing,
Noros,	Johnson,	Leach.
Dressler,	Ah Sam	
Görtz,		
Iversen.		

There were also dogs on the boats, and De Long's cutter towed a small dinghy with seven more dogs in it. Four of the dogs jumped overboard almost immediately and were lost.

Traveling by boat was much more efficient. On August 11,

they covered twenty miles, and some days they made as much as fifty. They camped on ice floes or the edges of islands, or simply caught snatches of sleep at sea. Food dwindled until they were left with only tea and pemmican. They drank the last of the lime juice. More dogs were lost at sea, and only Snoozer remained.

By September 4, they were trapped by rough ice again. Dragging the boats across meant "the hardest morning's work we have yet had." De Long sunk through the ice up to his shoulders. They stopped for the night on a long sandbar.

"Dimly through the snow the loom of mountains could be seen to the westward, but whether distant five miles or fifty I could not say," the captain wrote. They were closer than he thought: the sandbar was an extension of a larger island.

Despite a blinding snowstorm, De Long sent several groups to explore the island. He couldn't walk at all because of swollen feet and toes broken out with itchy irritations caused by exposure to cold, wet conditions.

The men found ruined huts and piles of old deer antlers— certain signs that people had been there at some point. In one hut, Alexey found a wooden drinking cup, a wooden spoon and fork, a mammoth tusk, and a small Russian coin dated 1840.

But they had no reason to stay on the island, so after a few days' rest they returned to the sea, where they were bombarded with waves and ice and had to bail nonstop. "The night was very dark, and the danger of our position was, owing to the floating pieces of ice, much increased," Newcomb recalled.

Finding empty huts like this one gave the men confidence that they'd soon reach an inhabited village.

"To have struck one of these ice pieces would have been death. Our escape was miraculous."

They took refuge on another island, a narrow strip of land where one of the men shot a deer. Each man was served a pound of fried meat with tea. A few hours later, they had an even bigger portion.

"This gave us a royal meal and finished the deer, except his bones, which we make soup of for dinner to-morrow," De Long wrote. "We have thus consumed since dinner-time eighty pounds of meat alone—no bones—a little more than two and one fourth pounds each, and are feeling comfortable and warm."

Melville advised De Long against any delay on the island. "Captain," he said, "miles would be better than meals." But De Long was convinced that the crew needed another day of recuperation. Melville warned that "a day's loss now, might count a week in the near future."

On September 12, an overnight snowfall blanketed the tents, and the temperature hovered near freezing. The ocean rolled with whitecaps, but little ice was seen. They launched the three boats and headed south.

After a morning of calm travel, the boats hauled up alongside an ice floe for a rest. They'd reached the southern edge of the ice, and before them lay a ninety-mile stretch of raging ocean. De Long hoped to make it to the mainland by late the following day.

They slowly ate their bits of pemmican. As one man noted later, "it was the last dinner we ever ate together."

The three boats separated in a tremendous gale on September 12, 1881.

CHAPTER 17

❖

Lost at Sea

The weather turned fierce. A heavy gale drove Melville's whaleboat nearly a thousand yards from De Long's as waves crashed over the sides. The boats were in danger of sinking, and none of the men could have survived in the icy water.

Melville eyed Danenhower, who'd been an outcast for

so long. The navigator was an expert in facing storms. "How can we get into a safe position?" Melville yelled.

"If we jibe twice," Danenhower replied, meaning to turn the boat by shifting the sail from side to side. Danenhower could barely see, but he could still read the waves.

"Take charge!" Melville called.

Danenhower jibed against the powerful wind and yelled at Herbert Leach to steer. Desperate to keep the whaleboat from sinking, the men bailed "for dear life" as Leach stood in the stern and worked the boat's tiller. The sails flapped wildly.

The waves grew higher, and the boat filled with water. "It seemed impossible that we could struggle longer in such a sea," Melville wrote. The men "clinging tenaciously to the foot of the sail suddenly found themselves steeped to their hips in icy water."

As difficult as it was for the crew of the whaleboat, the two cutters fared worse. Chipp's boat wasn't made to withstand such a storm, and De Long's was weighted down with two metal cases of the *Jeannette*'s books, specimens, and other items. De Long would have rather gone without food than part with his journal or other records of the voyage.

Somehow, the whaleboat drew close enough for Melville to call to De Long, but "a monstrous sea came combing onward and deluged both of us." Melville hollered that he "must run or swamp"—the first cutter's pace was too slow for safety. De Long waved him on, then yelled "some message which was lost in the noise of the gale."

Melville looked back at Chipp's struggling second cutter

and "saw her far off in the dim twilight rise full before the wind on the crest of a wave, and then sink briefly out of sight." It reappeared for a moment until "an immense sea enveloped her," Melville wrote. "I could discern a man striving to free the sail where it had jammed against the mast; she plunged again from view; and though wave after wave rose and fell, I saw nothing but the foam and seething white caps of the cold dark sea."

Chipp and De Long were gone from sight. For once unsure of himself, Melville asked Danenhower, "What now?"

"Steer with the wind," Danenhower said. "We can make good weather of it until dark."

As the boat rocked wildly, Jack Cole lashed three tent poles into a triangle and laced them with a canvas sheet to make a drag—a type of sea anchor.

Danenhower saw that the waves "ran in threes and that there was a short lull after the third and heaviest one." As the men rowed feverishly, Cole worked the sails. The boat was in danger of swamping, and Danenhower knew that they must turn and face the waves. "Lower away!" he shouted during the brief lull, signaling for Leach to turn the boat hard and for Cole to lower the sail.

"The boat came round, gave a tremendous dive, and she was then safe, head to sea," Danenhower wrote. "We eased the oars and launched the drag." But the drag wasn't heavy enough to hold them steady, so they pulled it in and attached a large copper pot.

Faint from hunger and thirst, the men worked all night to

remain in that position. Waves constantly came into the boat. "Everybody did his utmost," said Newcomb, "but it seemed as if every moment would be our last."

The crew kept bailing.

"I sat at the helm about fourteen hours before the wind abated enough for me to be relieved," Leach recalled. "When the time came I rose up and fell flat into the bottom of the boat. My feet were frozen stiff, and my legs were chilled up to my body so badly that I think they could have been taken off without my feeling it."

To relieve his mind from his thirst, Melville chewed a sliver of wood, "which induced a flow of saliva."

At daybreak, the storm still raged. Neither of the other boats was in view.

The ten men of the whaleboat looked at each other. Somehow, they'd survived an impossible ordeal. Could either of the cutters have made it through?

Their faces revealed the men's sad conclusion: it seemed likely that they were the only survivors of the *Jeannette.*

CHAPTER 18

Cursing Petermann

After ninety-six hours at sea, the whaleboat's crew finally collapsed on a beach, unsure of where they'd landed. It was September 16. Every inch of flesh was a "sodden and spongy" mass of blisters and sores. They had no drinkable water and very little food.

"We were wet through, and so stiff as scarcely to be able to walk," Newcomb remembered. "But we were ashore again on the big land, and that was enough."

Melville's last orders from De Long were to head for Cape Barkin, Siberia. If the other boats had somehow survived, they would go there, too. But as the men talked, "we speculated freely upon the fate of our companions; the general opinion being that ours was the only boat which outlived the gale." It made more sense to try to find a village nearby.

Danenhower estimated that they were "probably in a swamp river, either twenty or forty miles south of Barkin." At least one man believed they'd reached the Lena River. Melville wasn't sure.

The Lena is a three-thousand-mile river that empties into the ocean on the northern coast of Siberia. Its delta region is a huge maze of rushing streams, shallow bays, and swamps.

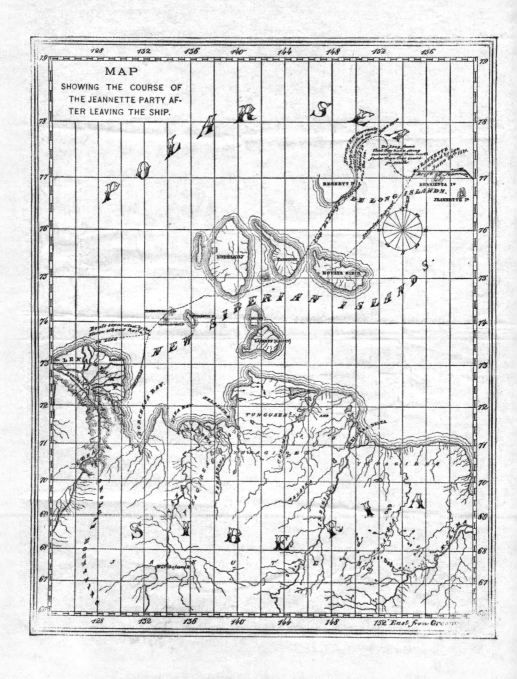

This map shows the route the crew followed after the *Jeannette* sank.

Melville believed that nomads "roamed all over the Delta." Petermann's chart showed many villages.

The men stumbled into an abandoned hut, desperate to restore circulation to their frozen hands and feet. But the warmth of a fire also brought back feeling within their bodies, and the men passed the night in agony, "as if millions of needles were piercing their limbs."

They sailed up the river for several days, and Melville became more convinced that they were in the Lena. But nothing they saw matched what was on the charts. "Bitterly we cursed Petermann and all his works which had led us astray," Melville wrote.

In scattered huts, the men found fish bones, reindeer antlers, and other signs that people had been there recently. They even saw human footprints, and Melville grew sure that rescue was not far off.

On September 19, a week after being separated from De Long and Chipp, the crew stopped to rest on a bleak, rocky riverbank. As they nibbled their pemmican, three canoes came into view. Each was paddled by a man.

Melville and Newcomb launched the whaleboat "to meet the strangers on equal terms." Melville called to them in English and German, but there was no sign that they understood. Soon all were laughing as Melville tried "to open up a conversation in every modern tongue of which I had the slightest smattering."

Two of the canoes moved away, but the youngest man paddled closer. Newcomb held out a bit of pemmican, then ate some himself to show that it wasn't poisoned. The young man took some and ate it.

Newcomb described the Siberian men in the same manner he'd taken note of the birds and insects he studied on the ice: "In stature they were small, complexion dark and swarthy, with straight black hair," he observed. "They had very good features, and were of comparatively happy dispositions." The men were members of the Tungus tribe, nomadic people who lived by hunting and fishing.

The young man's name was Tomat. He waved for the other canoes to join them, and all headed for shore. "Cushat, cushat," said Tomat. He pointed to the fish, venison, and a goose that the others were unloading from their canoes. *Cushat* meant "eat."

Melville made tea while the food cooked. He drew pictures and did his best to show the men that he needed to get to a village. His map showed that Bulun was the nearest settlement of any significant size.

"Soak, soak," said Tomat, shaking his head for "no." There was too much ice; the weather was too extreme. He fell to the ground and closed his eyes, pretending to be dead. Tomat knew that attempting a journey to Bulun under these conditions meant they all would "pomree"—die!

Instead, Tomat led them to a small, empty hunting camp up the river. He said he would go no farther.

Exasperated, Melville launched the whaleboat, hoping his crew could get to Bulun without a guide. But winter arrived in full force that night. By daybreak, the snowy landscape had changed so much that he "could barely distinguish" it any longer.

They had no choice but to return to the hunting camp.

When the weather cleared, Tomat guided them to a small, inhabited village, where they were stranded for several weeks by another onslaught of storms.

In early October, a convicted thief named Kusmah Eremoff came to the village. Years earlier, he'd been exiled to Siberia, a common punishment for Russian criminals. He claimed that he could make it to Bulun and alert Russian authorities that the *Jeannette* crew needed assistance.

Melville wrote letters to the secretary of the U.S. Navy and the U.S. minister in St. Petersburg, Russia. But he decided not to send them because he didn't trust Eremoff.

Eremoff said he'd return in five days. Melville waited in frustration for nearly a month. The Russian exile finally returned from Bulun on October 29, full of excuses for the delay. He handed Melville a note.

Melville opened "the dirty, crumpled scrap" and read it with astonishment.

Arctic steamer *Jeannette* lost on the 11th June; landed on Siberia 25th September or thereabouts; want assistance to go for the Captain and Doctor and (9) other men.

WILLIAM F. C. NINDEMANN,
LOUIS P. NOROS
Seamen, U.S.N.
Reply in haste: want food and clothing.

Nindemann and Noros had been in De Long's cutter. They were alive! Melville made immediate plans to reach them.

Members of De Long's party wade to shore in the Lena Delta.

CHAPTER 19

A Death March

After the two cutters and the whaleboat separated on September 12, De Long seemed to have lost much of his spirit. While his crew battled to stay afloat for a day and a half on the raging ocean, the captain climbed into his sleeping bag and barely moved. He complained to Dr. Ambler about his cold hands and feet, and developed "a nervous chuckle in his throat."

De Long made only a few notations in a small notebook until September 17, when the crew finally reached land. They found themselves in a muddy, treeless delta 120 miles west of the spot where Melville's whaleboat had gone ashore. De Long barely mentioned the other boats, except to note that they hadn't been seen.

He wrote a letter with the nub of a pencil and left it in an instrument box above the riverbank:

Monday, 19th of September, 1881.
LENA DELTA

The following named fourteen persons belonging to the Jeannette (which was sunk by the ice on June 12, 1881, in latitude N. 77° 15′, longitude E. 155°) landed here on the evening of the 17th inst. [of this month], and will proceed on foot this afternoon to try to reach a settlement on the Lena River: De Long, Ambler, Collins, Nindemann, Gortz, Ah Sam, Alexey, Ericksen, Kaack, Boyd, Lee, Iversen, Noros, Dressler.

A record was left about a half mile north of the southern end of Semenovski Island buried under a stake. The thirty-three persons composing the officers and crew of the Jeannette left that island in three boats on the morning of the 12th inst., (one week ago). That same night we were separated in a gale of wind, and I have seen nothing of them since. Orders had been given in event of such an accident for each boat to make the best of its way to a settlement on the Lena River before waiting for anybody. My boat made the land in the morning of the 16th inst., and I suppose we are at the Lena Delta. I have had no chance to get sights for position since I left Semenovski Island. After trying for two days to get inshore without grounding, or to reach one of the river mouths, I abandoned my boat, and we waded one and one half miles ashore, carrying our provisions and outfit with us. We must now try with God's help to walk to a settlement, the nearest of which I believe to be ninety-five miles distant. We are all well, have four days' provisions, arms and ammunition, and are carrying with us only ship's books and papers, with blankets, tents, and some medicines; therefore, our chances of getting through seem good.

GEORGE W. DE LONG,
Lieut. U. S. Navy Commanding.

Arctic Exploring Steamer Jeannette.

Thursday 22ᵗʰ of Sept 1881   Lat. _____   Long. _____

At a Hut on the Lena Delta
Believed to be near Tcholbogoje

The following named Persons, 14 of the Officers and Crew of the Jeannette reached this place yesterday afternoon on foot from the Arctic Ocean

George W DeLong   **Commander** of Expedition
Lieutenant U.S. Navy

P.A. Surgeon J.M. Ambler   Nelse Iverson — Adolph Dressler. H.H.Kaack
Dr J.J. Collins
W.F. Hendermann   L.P. Norris. Walter Lee. Mr. Sam — Aheey —
H.H. Erickson
A. Gortz
G.W. Boyd

☞ Whoever finds this paper is requested to forward it to the Secretary of the Navy, with a note of the time and place at which it was found.

☞ Quiconque trouvera ce papier est prié d'y marquer le temps et lieu où il l'aura trouvé, et de le faire parvenir au plutôt au Ministre de la Marine Americaine à Washington.

☞ Wer dieses Papier findet ist gebeten, dasselbe an den Secretär der Admiralität in Washington zu senden und Zeit und Ort anzugeben, wann und wo dasselbe gefunden.

The Jeannette was crushed and Sunk by the ice on the 12ᵗʰ of

☞ Quienquiera hallàra este papel, está pedido de enviarlo al Secretario del Almirantazgo, a Washington, con una nota del tiempo y del lugar en los quales se halló el dicho papel.

June 1881 in Lat N 77-15 Long E 155°.0′. After having drifted 22

☞ Enhver som finder dette papiir, anmodes at indsende samme ufortövet til Regjeringen i Kiöbenhavn eller i Stockholm, eller til Secretairen af det Admiralitet i Washington, med bemærkning angaaende tiden naar, og stedet hvor papiret er fundet.

months in the tremendous pack ice of this ocean — The entire 33 persons

☞ Een ieder, die dit papier mogt vinden, wordt hiermede verzogt, om het zelve, ten spoedigste, te willen zonden, aan den Heer Minister van de Marine der Nederlanden in 'S Gravenhage, of wel aan den Secretaris der Admiraliteit, te Washington, en daar by te voegen eene nota, inhoudende de tyd en de plaats alwaar dit papier it gevonden geworden.

comprising officers and crew dragged 3 boats

☞ Каждый кто найдетъ сей листъ, имѣетъ доставить оный безъ потери времени въ г. Вашингтонъ, Соед. Шт. Сѣв. Америки, Господину Секретарю Морскаго Департамента, означивъ на семъ листѣ время и мѣсто, когда и гдѣ оный былъ найденъ.

and provisions

Navy Department, Washington, D.C.
June 1st, 1879.

and the ice to Lat N 76°38′ Long 150°.30′ E where we landed upon a

33669.   E. & S.—2500.—3,74.

new island. Bennett Island — on the 29ᵗʰ July — From thence we proceeded sometimes in boat, sometimes dragging over ice, until the 10ᵗʰ September when we reached Semenovski Island about 90 miles NE of this Delta. We sailed from there in company on the 12ᵗʰ of

De Long left detailed notes like this one at several places along his route.

The men were sick and injured, with blue, frozen feet. But after two days of rest, they left the cutter behind and began walking. They didn't even bring their sleeping bags; instead, they cut them up to make foot coverings. But De Long made sure the ship's charts, logbooks, papers, and journals were hauled.

Their trip over land was much more difficult than the whaleboat's travels on the river. Stumbling and groaning with the heavy loads, the men needed three fifteen-minute rests during the first two hours.

Petermann's map was confusing and mislabeled. It showed a settlement named Sagastyr in two different places and did not show the larger village of North Bulun at all. So De Long aimed for the only nearby settlement that *was* on the map.

The captain finally agreed to stow a few of the books and records in a place where they could be retrieved if the men were ever rescued. Still, their progress was excruciatingly slow. Hans Ericksen, who had proved to be so strong when he accompanied Melville to Henrietta Island, "hobbled along a foot at a time," wrote De Long, who continued to confide in his notebook. "Every one of us seems to have lost all feeling in his toes, and some of us even half way up the feet," he noted. "That terrible week in the boat has done us a great injury."

William Nindemann stayed alongside his friend Ericksen and helped him walk. Both men were Europeans, Nindemann from Germany and Ericksen from Denmark.

Dr. Ambler wrote that Ericksen's feet "look very bad . . . but we must move on as every mile brings us nearer striking distance of a settlement. We cannot offer to carry him as all the men are loaded to their full strength, & as long as he can walk he will have to do so."

De Long kept his eye on poor Snoozer—the last remaining dog—who trotted by his side. The pemmican was almost gone, and except for one stringy seagull, they hadn't been able to shoot any game.

Snoozer could provide a couple of meals for the fourteen men. After that?

Ericksen collapsed on the trail. "I cannot go any further," he whispered to Nindemann. De Long scolded Ericksen and lifted him to his feet. Ambler declared that "no man will be left alone."

Ericksen hobbled for another mile. The men built a fire and spent a miserably cold night under a heavy snowfall. They had only one tent, but it couldn't possibly shelter all of the men. They cut it in half for two makeshift blankets.

The next day, fresh snow revealed a large number of reindeer tracks, which brightened the men's spirits. Even Ericksen was able to walk again, and by midafternoon they'd reached two empty huts. Was this the "settlement" on De Long's map? If so, they were nearly ninety miles from the next one!

De Long "concluded that this was a suitable place to halt the main body, and send on a couple of good walkers to make a forced march to get relief." The rest would stay behind "to eke out an existence" while waiting to be rescued.

De Long chose Nindemann and Dr. Ambler to leave the next morning. Thirteen men crawled into the huts. One stayed out.

Long after dark, De Long heard a familiar voice. "All asleep inside?"

Alexey's hunting skill provided De Long's group with lifesaving reindeer meat.

Alexey stuck his head into De Long's hut. He held out a hindquarter of meat. "Captain, we got two reindeer," the expert hunter said.

The grateful men "cried enough," and rebuilt the fire. Each was soon gobbling down a pound-and-a-half portion of Alexey's reindeer.

"The darkest hour *is* just before the dawn," wrote De Long, regaining his old enthusiasm. He rethought his plans. They had warm huts and fresh meat, so why send anyone ahead now?

The next morning, Nindemann, Alexey, and five other men dragged in the two reindeer. De Long figured they had enough meat for several days of recovery in the huts, and in the meantime they might shoot more game. He claimed that the ailing men were getting better, or at least no worse.

De Long took account of the meat: "Meat free from bone, fifty-four and a half pounds; meat on the bone, fourteen pounds; bones for soup, fifteen pounds."

All fourteen men set off together on September 24. De Long left behind his rifle "as a surprise to the next visitor." It was just too heavy to carry.

They forged along for a few rough miles a day. Ericksen developed a painful foot ulcer, exposing the muscles and tendons. The men were soon down to a handful of pemmican "and the dog." Then eleven deer came into sight, and only ten escaped.

"Saved again!" De Long proclaimed.

But the captain finally had to admit that Ericksen's life was in danger because of his infected feet. Forcing him to continue walking would probably kill him, but if they stayed put, they'd all likely die of starvation.

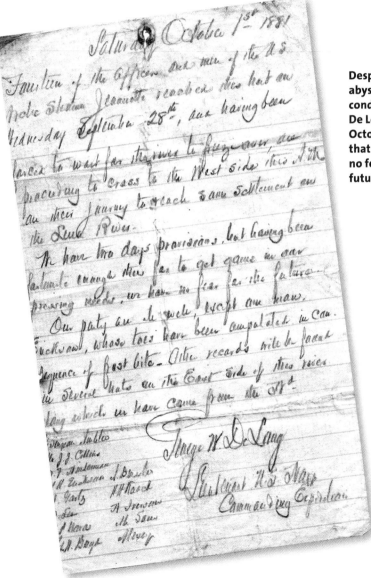

Despite the abysmal conditions, De Long wrote on October 1, 1881, that "we have no fear for the future."

De Long turned to Nindemann, his most reliable worker, and asked him to make a sled. Nindemann found a plank of wood. "I had nothing else but an old dull hatchet," he said, but he managed to construct a workable sled.

Dragging Ericksen, the men pressed forward. They found a hut and made a roaring fire. Ericksen groaned in his sleep, murmuring words in English, German, and his native Danish.

After they'd loaded up the next day, Nindemann went to the hut for Ericksen. Ten black nubs on the snow caught his attention. He looked at them closely, then stepped back as he recognized what they were. "I saw some toes lying outside of the hut," Nindemann recalled. Dr. Ambler had cut the dead, frostbitten digits from Ericksen's feet.

Snoozer died on October 3, victim of a carefully aimed gunshot. De Long could not bring himself to eat the resulting stew, though most of the men did.

Then Ericksen "departed this life" at 8:45 a.m. on October 6. The ground was frozen solid and there were no tools to dig with anyway. "The seaman's grave is the water," De Long said, "and therefore we will bury him in the river." They carried Ericksen out on the ice and "buried" him in a hole.

Nindemann carved these words into a board and fastened it on the hut where Ericksen died:

IN MEMORY
H. H. ERICKSEN,
Oct. 6, 1881,

U.S.S. Jeannette

Ericksen's clothing was shared by his shipmates, who also kept his Bible and locks of his hair. "Peace to his soul," wrote Ambler.

Without Ericksen, the men could move a little faster, but hunger and deep snow soon made walking almost impossible. More men were breaking down, and De Long feared that they'd soon join Ericksen.

"Nindemann, do you think you are strong enough to make a forced march" to the settlement? De Long asked.

"He told me I could take any man I wanted except Alexey," Nindemann recalled. Alexey was too valuable as a hunter; his skills provided the best chance the remaining men had of surviving. So Nindemann chose Louis Noros because Noros could "get over ground as well as any one."

"If you find assistance come back as quick as possible," De Long said, "and if you do not you are as well off as we are."

The men said a tearful good-bye, shaking hands with everyone and receiving three cheers. They trudged off through a foot and a half of fresh snow, carrying two blankets, a rifle, and forty rounds of ammunition, but no food.

Noros kept his eyes on "a high, conical, rocky island, which rose up out of the river." That landmark would help him remember where they'd left their companions.

De Long and the others limped forward for a few miles, following the tracks left by Nindemann and Noros. They prayed that those two would reach a settlement and send back help.

George W. De Long Journal

OCTOBER 10TH, MONDAY.

Eat deerskin scraps. Yesterday morning ate my deerskin foot-nips. . . . All hands weak and feeble, but cheerful. God help us.

OCTOBER 11TH, TUESDAY.

S. W. gale with snow. Unable to move. No game.

OCTOBER 12TH, WEDNESDAY.

For dinner we tried a couple of handfuls of Arctic willow in a pot of water and drank the infusion. . . . Hardly strength to get fire-wood.

OCTOBER 13TH, THURSDAY

We are in the hands of God, and unless He intervenes we are lost. We cannot move against the wind, and staying here means starvation. Afternoon went ahead for a mile, crossing either another river or a bend in the big one. After crossing, missed [Walter] Lee. Went down in a hole in the bank and camped. Sent back for Lee. He had turned back, lain down, and was waiting to die. All united in saying Lord's Prayer and Creed after supper. Living gale of wind. Horrible night.

CHAPTER 20

Dwindling Company

S urprisingly, Alexey was the second man to die, on October 17. He'd continued to hunt every day as his strength faded. "Exhaustion from hunger & exposure" was Dr. Ambler's final verdict.

Heinrich Kaack and Walter Lee both passed away on the twenty-first. De Long read "prayers for [the] sick" as the surviving men huddled in a hole in the snowbank.

De Long recorded the passing of the days, making occasional notes like "Suffering in our feet" and "A hard night." When they moved a few hundred yards up the riverbank, the men dragged along the two metal cases that held most of the *Jeannette*'s records. Nelse Iversen, Adolph Dressler, George Boyd, and Carl Görtz died there before the end of October.

Only the captain, the doctor, Jerome Collins, and Ah Sam remained. They had no food, very little clothing, and part of a tent to cover them in the bitter cold. Barely able to stand but still restless, De Long had Ambler and Ah Sam help him move the *Jeannette*'s records thirty feet up the bank to protect them from flooding.

Then they huddled together to wait.

Nindemann and Noros trudged for days through deep
snow and ice in an effort to reach a settlement.

Louis Noros

Nindemann and Noros had made slow progress, crossing shallow, ice-filled streams. They killed one ptarmigan, a bird about the size of a pigeon. They also ate a pair of sealskin pants.

The nights were desperately cold and stormy, and the two could only dig holes in the snow for shelter. "Noros now and then would fall off asleep," Nindemann said later. "I let him sleep for about five minutes, then called him, telling him to knock his feet together to keep them from freezing."

The men saw few signs of life, but finally they reached a hut with a mound of rotten fish. The fish was the texture of sawdust and a moldy blue, but they hadn't eaten anything for days. They filled their stomachs. The fish made them sick with severe diarrhea.

By then, they worried "that we were the only two men alive out of the whole expedition," Noros said. They knew they couldn't last much longer.

A crow flying overhead gave Nindemann a glimmer of hope. "This was always a sign up in the Arctic that when you see a crow . . . you generally find natives." A few days later, they did.

Their sickness had kept them confined to the hut with the moldy fish. They were surprised when the door opened, and their Native visitor was just as shocked to find the hut occupied. Communication proved difficult, but eventually the man and some others helped Nindemann and Noros get to the village of Bulun. The villagers also provided food, boots, and deerskin clothing.

Bulun was nothing more than "a lot of huts and some large boats," according to Nindemann. They met the village "commandant," and asked him for a pen and paper. Nindemann dictated a note to Noros, with the intention that it would be telegraphed to the American minister in St. Petersburg.

"At Bulun we tried to get a telegram sent, but could not make them understand," Noros said. There was no telegraph station in the village anyway.

The commandant said he would take care of sending the telegram. Nindemann and Noros found a "dirty and miserable" hut to recuperate in. They were still weak from diarrhea.

Several days passed. "On the evening of November the 3d, I was laying in bed; Noros was sitting on the table looking toward the door," Nindemann recalled. "I heard the door open, and looking round I saw a man coming in the door that was dressed up in fur clothes."

Nindemann paid little attention until he heard the visitor speak. "Hello, Noros," the man said, "you are alive."

Nindemann jumped up. He might as well be seeing a ghost.

Their visitor was George W. Melville.

CHAPTER 21

"False Hopes"

Melville winced as he looked around the filthy hut where Nindemann and Noros rested. "Both were so sick as to be barely able to walk, vomiting and purging violently," he recalled.

Melville pried whatever information he could from his emaciated shipmates. They told him that a well-equipped dogsled team could reach De Long and the others in three days. But they tearfully added that more than three weeks had passed since they'd left their starving companions. It would have taken a miracle for them to survive that long. On the other hand, they'd all survived against incredible odds already. So there was hope.

Melville made immediate plans to search, even though his legs were swollen and blistered from frostbite. There was no way Nindemann and Noros could join him. Both were near death. Melville found them a larger hut and made arrangements for better food and care, insisting that the U.S. government would eventually pay the villagers for the food and shelter.

Melville organized a team of Tungus guides and dogsled

drivers. He wrote notes to the U.S. minister in St. Petersburg, the London office of the *New York Herald*, and the secretary of the Navy in Washington, D.C. In his notes, Melville promised to conduct a "vigorous and constant search" and demanded funding for the trip. He sent the notes off with a messenger to have them telegraphed.

The nearest telegraph station to Bulun was three thousand miles to the southwest in the small Siberian city of Irkutsk. That's as far as New York City is from Los Angeles. The trip by dogsled would take at least six weeks.

Melville wouldn't wait a day. He prepared to head into the Lena Delta in search of De Long with the help of the Tungus men.

By then, the rest of the whaleboat crew had also arrived in Bulun. Melville ordered James Bartlett to stay there in case Melville himself needed to be rescued later. He sent the rest of the crewmen to the larger village of Yakutsk.

Melville was welcomed by Siberian Natives and spent several nights in villages like this one while searching for De Long.

On November 9, Melville reached a hut where Nindemann and Noros had slept after leaving De Long. But the dogsled drivers refused to go farther. "Soak, soak," one said. *No, no.*

"Why not?" Melville asked.

"Cushat soak" was the reply. *Nothing to eat.*

How could that be? Melville had purchased ten days' worth of frozen fish. They'd only been traveling for four!

The dogsled drivers insisted on returning to their village. Melville fired his rifle over their heads. No one is going back, he shouted.

"They explained that there had been a famine and I had taken all the fish in the village," Melville wrote. Eighty village dogs had already died of starvation and the people were in danger, too. So the villagers had taken most of the fish back after loading it on the sleds.

Melville threatened to eat the dogs if he faced starvation. "And after they are eaten, I will eat you!"

He ordered the Tungus guides to continue through the snow. Because Melville had the only gun, they obeyed the weak, surly man, who was confined to a sled. "I was now so badly lamed as to be utterly unable to stand up without assistance," Melville wrote.

They ate "deer bones with tendons and a little ragged meat attached" that they found in huts, and also some deer hooves, which grew soft when roasted. The dogs ate rotten geese skins and feet.

Melville forced the guides to take him to the nearest village to get more food. The village was far out of the way, but the detour paid off. Villagers showed Melville three notes they'd collected in huts along the river. All were written by De Long, noting the group's progress and state of health. Melville pieced together a trail from De Long's information. One note told where De Long had stashed some of the logbooks, navigation equipment, and other items. Melville ordered the sled drivers to take him there through a driving blizzard. He found the cache.

Melville vowed to search for his shipmates "until I found them dead or alive." The drivers rebelled again—the weather was too harsh to continue.

Melville knew the snow had obliterated the landmarks Nindemann and Noros had sketched for him. There was just too much snow and wind. "The natives were wise in admonishing me that I should die too if I persisted in searching at that season of the year," Melville wrote. So he returned to Bulun, arriving on December 30, 1881. He estimated that he'd covered more than one thousand miles in his search.

Melville was surprised to find not just Bartlett but Nindemann, Noros, and three other crewmen still in Bulun. They hadn't found transportation so had stayed behind while Danenhower and the others traveled to Yakutsk. Melville made travel arrangements, and before long, he and the others were all in Yakutsk, where they spent part of the winter in relative comfort.

While recuperating there, Melville received responses to his earlier telegrams. Bennett pledged money for the search. He'd also sent a *Herald* reporter to Siberia, although he didn't tell that to Melville.

When Melville received this telegram from the secretary of the Navy, he made immediate preparations for his second attempt to find De Long:

OMIT NO EFFORT, SPARE NO EXPENSE, IN SECURING SAFETY OF MEN. . . . LET THE SICK AND THE FROZEN OF THOSE ALREADY RESCUED HAVE EVERY ATTENTION, AND AS SOON AS PRACTICABLE HAVE THEM TRANSFERRED TO A MILDER CLIMATE. DEPARTMENT WILL SUPPLY NECESSARY FUNDS.

HUNT, SECRETARY.

Nindemann was back on his feet, so Melville brought him and Bartlett along when he returned to Bulun in mid-February. In the meantime, Bennett's reporter caught up with Danenhower in Yakutsk and spent several days interviewing him "off the record." In other words, Danenhower did not expect his words to be published in newspapers around the world.

Danenhower complained that he'd been mistreated by De Long and Ambler, claiming that he'd been perfectly able to work all the time. His eye trouble, he lied, was caused by a cold virus, and the glare from the ice had aggravated it. Danenhower also questioned many of De Long's other decisions, and he objected to being under Melville's command in the whaleboat.

The *Herald* published long excerpts from the interviews. The paper also printed a false article that said the entire crew of the *Jeannette* had been found alive. And Bennett sent a telegram

Thirteen survivors of the *Jeannette* gathered in the Siberian village of Yakutsk for the winter. Shown here, back row, from left: Raymond Newcomb, Herbert Leach; center row: John Lauterbach, George Melville, Aneguin; bottom row: William Nindemann, Frank Mansen. (The others in Yakutsk were Louis Noros, Henry Wilson, Charles Tong Sing, John Danenhower, James Bartlett, and Jack Cole.)

to Emma De Long with the blatant lie that "Commander De Long has reached the mouth of the Lena safely and is now well and looking after the sick members of the expedition."

Emma was suspicious. "If George was safe why had he not telegraphed me himself?" she wondered. She wrote her husband a letter, not to "nowhere" this time but via the U.S. minister in Moscow. She offered to travel to Siberia if George was sick and needed her help. "It seems so unnatural for you not to speak for yourself," Emma wrote to her husband. She soon realized that Bennett "entirely misled me."

Bennett apologized that his telegram had "raised false hopes," but he insisted that De Long would be found safe. While rival newspapers speculated that all of De Long's group was dead, the *Herald* continued to paint a rosier picture about the *Jeannette* and its commander:

After cleaving her poleward way through more than a thousand miles of the frozen ocean she has succumbed to its resistless forces, perhaps at the very time when leaving her winter quarters, her commander was about to make a still further advance toward the extreme north. However deplorable the disaster which arrested the movements he returns home with tidings of a large area of the polar ocean never before seen by man.

Other papers reported the truth: that, on De Long's command, Nindemann and Noros had left the others freezing and starving, with Ericksen already dead.

"All this forms a dreadful picture for me to dwell upon," Emma wrote, "and I do not know whether I will ever see my own dearest husband again or not."

CHAPTER 22

"The Siberian Winds"

Melville was determined to reach the spot where he'd ended his search months earlier. He relied on Nindemann's memory of the area, and on Bartlett's strength. But Siberia is vast, and the winter weather severe. "To the southward of the mountain range absolute stillness reigned, and the snow-fall was constant and heavy," Melville wrote. But as they traveled north, "I at once felt a change in the atmosphere. Whereas to the southward everything was as calm as the quiet of death, in front of us a gale was already blowing."

It took the men three weeks to reach Bulun, where they were stormed in for another month. They finally set out in miserable conditions. Snow was piled so high that Nindemann couldn't recognize the terrain. Eventually they reached the high, rocky island that Noros had identified as a landmark. On March 24, Nindemann spotted a broken flatboat near the river. This was the spot where he and Noros had first camped.

Nearby, four poles stuck out of a snowbank. They were lashed together, and a Remington rifle hung from the lashing. Melville ran toward it and fell, cutting his face. He recognized the rifle as Alexey's.

Melville and Nindemann found De Long's body partly covered by snow.

Minutes later, Melville discovered a firebed on a slope. He bent to pick up a copper kettle from the snow, and "I caught sight of three objects at my very feet; and one of these, the one I was about to step over—*was the hand and arm* of a body raised out of the snow."

Melville instantly recognized De Long's coat. "He lay on his right side, with his right hand under his cheek, his head pointing north, and his face turned to the west," Melville wrote. "His feet were drawn slightly up as though he were sleeping; his left arm was raised with the elbow bent, and his hand, thus horizontally lifted, was bare."

A few feet behind De Long, Melville found the small note-book, or ice journal, in which the captain had recorded his most recent entries. With his final bit of strength, De Long apparently threw it back to ensure that it didn't burn in the fire. He never lowered his arm.

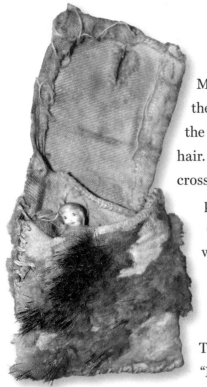

In the pockets of De Long's coat, Melville found two pairs of eyeglasses, the captain's silver watch, a whistle, and the blue pouch with the lock of Emma's hair. The pouch also held Emma's gold cross set with three pearls and the little porcelain doll De Long had purchased in Alaska for Sylvie. The doll was wrapped in a tiny blanket.

Melville started reading from the back of De Long's journal, learning the order in which the men had died. The last entry, dated October 30, said "Mr. Collins dying."

A few feet from De Long's body, Ah Sam lay faceup with his hands across his chest. He'd probably been placed that way by the captain and the doctor. He wore a pair of red knit socks with the heels and toes worn away. Few of

TOP: **Among De Long's possessions when he died was this tiny porcelain doll he'd purchased in Alaska for his daughter.**

BOTTOM: **De Long recorded the deaths of his crew on the final page of his journal.**

Tuesday October 25th
135th day.
    Wednesday October 26th
136th day.

    Thursday October 27th.
137th day,   Iveson broken dorm.
    Friday October 28th.
138th day. Iveson died during early morning.
    Saturday Oct 29.
139th day Dressler died during night
    Sunday Oct 30 –
140th day . Boyd & Gertz died during night – dr Collins dying

the other bodies had any footwear. Most had bits of blanket or tent tied with ropes around their limbs, in an attempt to keep from freezing.

A medicine case and a few other items were scattered about, including the four-foot cylinder that held the ship's charts and drawings.

Other bodies were found beneath the snow. Their clothing was scorched from lying so close to the fire. Collins clutched a rosary.

Dr. Ambler appeared to have died last. He gripped De Long's pistol, which he'd taken from the dead captain to protect himself or to kill an animal for food if one came to feast on the bodies. Melville noticed blood on Ambler's mouth and beard, and wondered if he'd shot himself. But there was no wound other than a small one on his hand. As he was dying of thirst, Ambler had bitten into his own thumb for liquid. "There he kept his lone watch to the last," Melville wrote, "on duty, on guard, under arms."

Melville discovered this letter that the dying doctor had written to his family:

On the Lena,
THURSDAY, OCT. 20TH, 1881.
To Edward Ambler, Esqr.
I write these lines in the faint hope that by God's merciful providence they may reach you all at home. I have myself now very little hope of surviving. We have been without food for nearly 2 weeks, with the exception

of 4 ptarmigans amongst 11 of us. We are growing weaker, and for more than a week have had no food. We can barely manage to get wood enough now to keep warm & in a day or two that will be passed. I write my brother to you all, my Mother, Sister, Brother Cary & his wife & family, to assure you of the deep love I now & have always borne you. If it had been God's will for me to have seen you all again I had hoped to have enjoyed the peace of home living once more. My mother knows how my heart has been bound to hers since my earliest years. God bless her on earth & prolong her life in peace & comfort. May his blessing rest upon you all. As for myself, I am resigned & bow my head in submission to the Divine Will. . . .

Your loving brother,

J.M. Ambler

No such letter from De Long was found. A page was missing from the captain's notebook, but if he'd written a letter to Emma on it, it was lost. Melville searched for the missing page. He later told Emma that "he firmly believed it carried a message" for her.

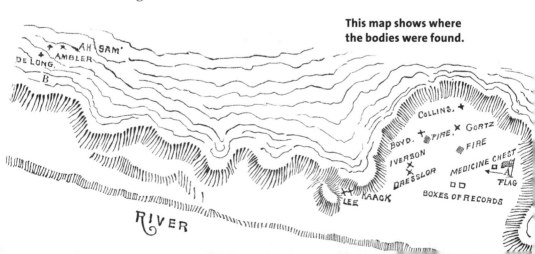

This map shows where the bodies were found.

**Melville, Nindemann, and Bartlett created this
temporary tomb for the bodies of their shipmates.**

"No doubt the Siberian winds had snatched it from my
husband's grasp," Emma wrote. "It was never found."

De Long's notes showed that they were still alive at least
ten days after Ambler wrote the letter. His final entry is dated
Sunday, October 30, the 136th day since the company began
walking away from the site of the *Jeannette*'s sinking. De Long
wrote that Collins was dying. That would have left Ah Sam
and Dr. Ambler as his only companions.

Melville, Nindemann, and Bartlett uncovered all the bodies
except Ericksen and Alexey, the two men buried in the river.
They tied everyone's personal items in small bundles and
labeled them. Then they made a temporary coffin from the
broken flatboat and created a tomb for the men. Eventually,
the bodies were transported to the United States.

It wasn't until May that Melville's next telegram reached the offices of the *New York Herald*. It was published in the following day's edition:

LENA DELTA, MARCH 24, 1882

    I HAVE FOUND LIEUT. DE LONG AND HIS PARTY; ALL DEAD.

    ALL THE BOOKS AND PAPERS HAVE ALSO BEEN FOUND.

    I REMAIN TO CONTINUE THE SEARCH FOR THE PARTY UNDER LIEUT. CHIPP.

MELVILLE

Melville scoured the delta for any remains of Chipp, his crew, and the second cutter. That search proved fruitless. He finally returned home to the United States more than three years after first departing for the Arctic.

The *New York Herald* reported the grim news of the men's deaths.

DE LONG AND HIS MEN DEAD

THEIR BODIES FOUND AT THE LENA DELTA.

ENGINEER MELVILLE'S BRIEF ANNOUNCEMENT OF HIS DISCOVERY—ALL THE BOOKS AND PAPERS RECOVERED—THE LOST EXPLORERS AND THEIR SUFFERINGS.

From the Herald of This Morning.

IRKUTSK, May 5.—The following dispatch has just reached here from Iakutsk:

LENA DELTA, March 24, 1882.

I have found Lieut. De Long and his party; all dead.

All the books and papers have also been found.

I remain to continue the search for the party under Lieut. Chipp.   MELVILLE.

The news of the loss of the Jeannette was received in this City on the night of Dec. 20 last. It was conveyed in a dispatch to the Russian Government from the Governor at Iakutsk and dated Dec. 19. Subsequent dispatches from Engineer Melville showed that after the wreck of the Jeannette the crew embarked in two cutters and a whale-boat. The boats were separated in a gale while in t

CHAPTER 23

---◆---

Homecoming

On the afternoon of September 13, 1882, the most courageous man in the United States strolled along the deck of the S.S. *Parthia* as the ocean liner steamed into New York Harbor. Surviving the harsh conditions in the Arctic, then risking his life again to search for De Long and the crew, had catapulted George W. Melville to world-hero status. Newspapers declared that every American recognized the forty-one-year-old engineer's bravery.

When Melville heard the sharp whistles of the tugs celebrating his arrival, he climbed up the ship's railing and threw his cap into the air. His long hair was grayer than it was when he'd boarded the *Jeannette* in the summer of 1879, and there was less of it. But he was finally home, exactly a year and a day after the storm had separated his boat from De Long's and Chipp's. His courage and perseverance after that tragic day had been well documented in New York City's many newspapers, including Bennett's *Herald*, the *New York Times*, and the *Evening Telegram*.

Nindemann and Noros were also on board, but the crowds in the harbor clamored for a sight of the engineer, chanting, "We want Melville!"

Melville waved and smiled, but he said little to the

spectators or reporters. He knew that the U.S. Congress had already directed a Navy Court of Inquiry to investigate the wreck of the *Jeannette* and the subsequent deaths. He'd save the details for his testimony before the committee.

The men had missed a lot. In the three years they were away, the United States had three presidents. Rutherford B. Hayes was still serving when the *Jeannette* departed in 1879, but he did not seek reelection. James A. Garfield was elected in 1880, but he'd been assassinated after just two hundred days in office. Garfield's vice president, Chester A. Arthur, was now president.

Thomas Edison's revolutionary electric lamps—like the ones that Jerome Collins had bungled up on the *Jeannette*— now illuminated much of New York City. Telephones had become more widespread.

Melville hoisted himself onto a little Navy tug moored beside the *Parthia*, where he was greeted by loved ones and friends. Seeing them after all he'd been through, the usually stoic Melville couldn't stop crying. Soon he sat quietly on a camp stool holding the arm of Emma De Long's father, recounting the gory details of the expedition as tears rolled down his frost-weathered face.

Then Melville rushed up the gangplank of the *Parthia* and collected two boxes. They held Captain De Long's most precious possessions—his journals and logbooks. Melville had guarded them fiercely for the past six months. He instructed a carriage driver to load up the boxes and drive him to the home of Emma De Long.

Melville had plenty of good reasons to keep a close eye on De Long's journals and other material. Unscrupulous reporters from Bennett's *New York Herald* had hounded him in Siberia, hoping the journals would reveal a story even more sensational than the known facts. Melville had risked his life to find his crewmates, and De Long had led a courageous expedition for the benefit of science and humanity. But the reporters were hoping to uncover mutiny, cannibalism, perhaps even murder. One had even dug up the temporary grave Melville and the others had built for De Long and his crew on the first cutter, searching the bodies for signs of cannibalism. Another reporter had intercepted a message from Melville intended for U.S. Navy officials. In it, Melville provided information about his discovery of De Long and the others and where they were entombed. That information had been widely published in papers throughout the country.

Melville was fully prepared to testify before the Court of Inquiry to prove that he had done all he could to find his shipmates alive and that the captain hadn't been a reckless commander. As he handed De Long's journals and logbooks to Emma, he knew that they would be key evidence.

Emma, of course, had been devastated when she learned months before of her husband's death. "It was as if the seas had closed over me," she wrote. But by the time Emma met with Melville, she'd found the emotional strength to defend her husband's honor and the dignity of the crew. She was determined to write about the voyage and publish the logbooks and journals. She was also willing to testify in court, gaining courage from Melville's words: "I will stand by you and De Long while I have a piece of ice to stand on."

The night of his arrival in New York, a carriage dropped off Melville at a restaurant for a banquet in his honor. Next to him sat Noros and Nindemann. Both were clean shaven, except for handlebar mustaches, and both said very little. Duck, oysters, and the finest steaks were on the menu, a huge change from the rotten fish, deer hooves, and sealskin clothing they'd eaten to stay alive.

After supper, as the air filled with the smoke of cigars and the clinking of champagne glasses, Melville was asked to speak to the hundreds of guests about the ordeal. Melville explained that he preferred to say nothing at all. Then he quickly changed his mind. "I feel that we did our whole duty," he told the crowd, "that we did all that we could do, and that if we had not tried to do that we would have been no men at all."

A few years later, Melville went to sea aboard the U.S.S. *Thetis*, and while on board he wrote an account of the *Jeannette* expedition. In that book, he told this story that captured the spirit and heart of the crew:

"On the day when the Jeannette sank, her bows were thrown upward, the ice ceased for a spell its fierce intent to crush her; and as the sun was shining brightly, De Long requested me to make a photograph of the doomed ship. So I set up the camera."

Melville went on board to develop the photo in the ship's darkroom, "using my watch to time the plate." When the call came to abandon ship, Melville stopped what he was doing, put the watch in his pocket, and rushed onto the ice. Later, he decided to leave the watch behind on the ice, but crew member Walter Lee said he would gladly take it. "If we ever get back to the United States I will return it to you," Lee said.

Lee carried the watch on the long march to Siberia.

"Lee was not very sure-footed," Melville wrote, "he had been shot through both hips during our civil war, and now kept tumbling into the water—and such water!—with almost intentional regularity. Of course the old single-cased watch came in for its share of the wettings, and at each one Lee would calmly empty it of the salt sea wave. And still it continued to keep time; albeit the rusting of its iron and steel parts soon streaked and stained the golden face, rim, and back."

One day, as the men crossed an open lead of water on an ice raft, Lee was knocked down. The impact smashed the watch's crystal and broke its hands. "I laughed and told him to throw the watch away," Melville wrote. "But no, he said, it was a great pleasure to the men to be told the time of day."

Alfred Sweetman, one of the carpenters, made a wooden case for the watch, "and Lee with his sheath-knife cut a tin hand and drove it down on the hour spindle, and all was well again." Lee could tell time well enough with just an hour hand, "for a minute hand is a frivolous luxury in the Arctic Circle."

When the men at last reached open water at the edge of the ice pack, Melville took possession of the watch again, since no one else on the whaleboat had one. The watch had to be wound every three hours or so, but it worked.

Months later, in Siberia, a political exile known as the "Little Blacksmith" secured a brass plate to the rim of the crystal, and an actual watchmaker added a new minute hand. But during Melville's search of the Lena Delta for De Long, "I discovered that the faithful old ticker did not tick as well as it did before the exile had it to repair, and upon opening the case I found that one of the jewels was gone. The little rogue had stolen the stone and replaced it with a piece of brass. . . . I had to ease or compress one of the screws in order to regulate the running of the watch."

Melville decided that the watch was another casualty of the Arctic, "and I despaired of its future usefulness."

"Finally, arriving at Philadelphia, I laid it away as a relic, but a certain sympathetic friend decided that it should be cleaned and put in order once again. Now it is fair to look upon; the rust stains have departed its poor old face; and as I write these words in the wardroom of the steamer *Thetis*, it is at sea once more, bound on another Arctic voyage."

EPILOGUE

⟨⟩

Thirty-three men embarked on the *Jeannette*'s Arctic journey to reach the North Pole. Twelve survived.

Most of the survivors testified during the Navy Court of Inquiry hearings to investigate the ship's sinking, rescue efforts, and conduct of the officers and crew. Although John Danenhower may have told reporters "off the record" in Siberia that he disagreed with De Long's

TOP: **Only people with tickets could attend De Long's funeral service.**

BOTTOM: **De Long's funeral procession—on February 22, 1884—drew huge crowds in New York City.**

35 Centre Aisle

ADMIT BEARER
—TO—
FUNERAL SERVICES
OF THE LATE
Lieut. Com. G. W. De Long,
AND COMRADES,
CHURCH OF THE HOLY TRINITY,
Madison Avenue and 42d Street.

After their deaths, Alexey and Aneguin were honored with these medals from the U.S. Congress for their skills and bravery.

decisions, on the witness stand he spoke highly of the captain and crew (except for Jerome Collins, who nearly everyone agreed was a troublemaker). Satisfied with the testimonies, top Navy officials concluded that the *Jeannette* had been well prepared and managed, noting that the crew "seems to have been a marvel of cheerfulness, good-fellowship, and mutual forbearance, while the constancy and endurance with which they met the hardships and dangers that beset them entitle them to great praise."

De Long's honor was confirmed, along with that of the crew and officers. That included George Melville, who was later promoted to engineer in chief, the highest rank an engineer could achieve in the Navy.

After the inquiry, Danenhower continued as a U.S. Navy officer. He married and had a family. But he also continued to battle his mental health disorder, stubbornly believing that he could handle it without medical help. Eventually, he could not. Danenhower killed himself in 1887.

Raymond Newcomb gave up stuffing birds and other wildlife specimens. He spent the rest of his career as the clerk of the board of health in his hometown of Salem, Massachusetts.

Louis Noros delivered mail for the U.S. Postal Service in

Fall River, Massachusetts, not far from where Newcomb lived. Noros obviously enjoyed walking, even after his Arctic ordeal.

The *Jeannette*'s answer to Hercules, William Nindemann made one more trip to the Arctic, then worked for a company that built submarines. As De Long had recommended in his logbook, Nindemann received the Congressional Medal of Honor for working tirelessly to mend the ship and keep it afloat.

When the *Jeannette* finally did sink, Aneguin helped his shipmates stay alive with his expert hunting skills. He survived the harrowing journey through the Arctic and into Siberia with Melville. But two months after his group made it safely to a Siberian village, Aneguin died of smallpox. Aneguin and Alexey—another hero of the expedition—were honored with special Congressional medals.

Emma De Long made good on her promise and published her husband's journals. She also wrote a best-selling memoir, *Explorer's Wife*, which lovingly describes her time with De Long and provides great insight into his character. She also made sure that her husband's remains were brought back from Siberia, in 1884. Emma never remarried and lived to be ninety. She's buried next to her husband in Woodlawn Cemetery in Brooklyn, New York.

Although De Long worried that the *Jeannette*'s scientific contributions had gone down with the ship, he must have carried a glimmer of hope that they'd accomplished something. Why else would he have lugged those large, heavy logbooks over hundreds of miles of ice?

De Long's detailed observations of weather, temperature, astronomy, ocean depths, animals and plants, and the westward drift of the ice pack revealed just how much the *Jeannette* expedition did accomplish. They'd also disproved faulty information about the Arctic, including the idea of an open polar sea. And De Long and his crew discovered three new islands (Jeannette, Henrietta, and Bennett), claiming them for the United States.

Three years after the *Jeannette* sank, Inuit fishermen spotted a large ice floe littered with objects off the southern coast of Greenland. They retrieved what they could, including a tent and a pair of sealskin trousers labeled LOUIS NOROS. The articles—abandoned by De Long and his crew after the ship was crushed by ice—had drifted 4,500 miles to the opposite side of the Arctic Ocean.

Explorers build on others' success and failures, and so Norwegian explorer Fridtjof Nansen was more interested in how far the ice floe had drifted than the articles it carried. Nansen figured that the floe had reached the North Pole on its westerly drift before reaching Greenland. That convinced Nansen that the way to navigate to the pole was to become locked in ice and drift to it.

Nansen had a wooden schooner built, called the *Fram*, with a thick, rounded hull that wouldn't be crushed by ice. In 1895, he nearly reached the North Pole by following the same route as the *Jeannette* and inched closer than De Long or any explorer before him. Nansen and his crew survived the three-year trek and returned home as heroes. But they hadn't reached the pole. It wasn't until 1909 that Robert Peary and Matthew Henson finally did.

One hundred and thirty-one years after the *Jeannette* sailed out of San Francisco harbor, the logbooks that Captain De Long saved were transcribed by citizen scientists. They'd volunteered for a weather project created by the National Oceanic and Atmospheric Administration (NOAA). With the Arctic climate rapidly transforming (ice is melting at an alarming rate), NOAA scientists realized that data recorded by early Arctic explorers could help determine the rate of climate change. Now climate scientists who log into weather-research sites can find De Long's ice measurements—some of the oldest on record—along with Newcomb's bird sightings, key information in the study and history of the polar region.

Ironically, the theory that led to the *Jeannette*'s demise—that the Arctic held an open polar sea—might someday become a reality because of global warming. Explorers have unwittingly contributed to that warming. But maybe that tide will change. The *political* climate is the greatest obstacle to fixing the *actual* climate, and it will take great courage and perseverance for forward-thinking leaders to overcome this and other obstacles. Heroes have stepped up throughout history to accomplish incredible things, just like De Long and his crew.

"If men must die, why not in honorable pursuit of knowledge?" George Melville once said. "Woe, woe, to America when the young blood of our nation has no sacrifice to make for science."

A NOTE FROM THE AUTHORS

——◆——

One of the thrills of research is the opportunity to hold pieces of history in your hands. It was one thing to know that De Long and his men had hauled his forty-five-pound journals over hundreds of miles of ice, somehow kept them safe while battling tumultuous, icy ocean waves, and lugged them across the muddy and bewildering Lena Delta through blizzards and gales. It was quite another experience to page through those actual journals, to read De Long's handwritten entries, and to imagine the crucible he'd been through.

And then to weigh that against the lock of his wife's hair and the tiny doll he'd purchased for his daughter, which he also carried with him through that entire ordeal.

We had the privilege of viewing and handling those artifacts and others on a research trip to the U.S. Naval Academy Museum in Annapolis, Maryland. The museum houses a substantial collection of material related to the *Jeannette*.

Another major boon to our research was discovering the Arctic exploration collection at Dartmouth College. The collection was the personal research library of Arctic explorer Vilhjalmur Stefansson, a Canadian who taught polar studies at Dartmouth in the early twentieth century. It includes original newspaper clippings unavailable at other libraries.

Reading reports from geographic societies about the *Jeannette* during its disappearance put the magnitude of the expedition into context. And, like the Naval Academy Museum, the Dartmouth library afforded us the chance to hold and read primary material from the *Jeannette*, including an S.O.S. message De Long left in a hut on the Lena Delta.

Thanks to the staffs at Dartmouth and the Naval Academy for their knowledge and hospitality and for providing us with copious amounts of research material.

Thanks also to several people who helped us track down correct information about Yup'ik hunters Alexey and Aneguin. In previously published books and articles, the two men have consistently been misidentified as Inuit (or Indian). Tribal coordinator Emily Kobuk of the Native Village of St. Michael checked census records that yielded valuable information. Erin Wahl, Robert Drozda, and Robyn Russell of the Alaska and Polar Regions Collections and Archives at the University of Alaska Fairbanks provided important guidance. They also

De Long kept detailed notes in these journals, then he and his crew lugged them all the way to Siberia.

pointed us toward Kenneth Pratt of the U.S. Bureau of Indian Affairs in Anchorage, who manages the largest existing collection of records on Alaska Native history and cultures. Pratt explained that "Alexey" was a name "assigned" by non-Native explorers. Unfortunately, Alexey's and Aneguin's Yup'ik names are lost to history.

Thanks, always, to our laser-eyed Calkins Creek editor, Carolyn P. Yoder, who commits to our stories as fully as we do (her weekend e-mails at 5:00 a.m. are proof of that). A big appreciation to Sue Cole and the Highlights production and design teams for making the historic images we found look great.

And thanks to our agent, Liza Voges, who has an incredible knack for finding the perfect home for the projects we love.

De Long's rifle (shown on p. 173), pencil, and eyeglasses and case were recovered with his frozen body.

BIBLIOGRAPHY

Books

Brandt, Anthony, ed. *The North Pole: A Narrative History.* Washington, DC: National Geographic, 2005.

Brooks, Charles Wolcott. *Early Migrations: Arctic Drift and Ocean Currents; Illustrated by the Discovery on an Ice-Floe off the Coast of Greenland of Relics from the American Arctic Steamer* Jeannette. San Francisco: Geo. Spaulding, 1884.

Brooks, Charles Wolcott. *Scientific Inferences, from a Certain State of Facts, as to the Probable Movements and Present Position of the American Arctic Exploring Yacht* Jeannette. . . . San Francisco: Proceedings of the California Academy of Sciences, 1880.

Danenhower, John Wilson. *Lieutenant Danenhower's Narrative of the* Jeannette. Boston: James R. Osgood, 1882.

De Long, Emma Wotton. *Explorer's Wife.* New York: Dodd, Mead, 1938.

De Long, Emma, ed. *The Voyage of the* Jeannette: *The Ship and Ice Journals of George W. De Long.* 2 vols. Boston: Houghton, Mifflin, 1883–84.

Fitzhugh, William W., and Susan A. Kaplan. *Inua: Spirit World of the Bering Sea Eskimo.* Washington, DC: Smithsonian Institution Press, 1982.

Gatewood, J. D., ed. *The Private Journal of James Markham Ambler, M.D.* Washington, DC: U.S. Navy Bureau of Medicine and Surgery Office of Medical History Collection, 1914.

Gilder, William H. *Ice-Pack and Tundra: An Account of the Search for the* Jeannette *and a Sledge Journey Through Siberia.* London: Sampson Low, Marston, Searle and Rivington, 1883.

Guttridge, Leonard F. *Icebound: The* Jeannette *Expedition's Quest for the North Pole*. Annapolis, MD: U.S. Naval Institute Press, 1986.

Hoehling, A. A. *The* Jeannette *Expedition: An Ill-Fated Journey to the Arctic*. New York: Abelard-Schuman, 1967.

Melville, George W. *In the Lena Delta*. Boston: Houghton, Mifflin, 1885.

Muir, John. *The Cruise of the* Corwin: *Journal of the Arctic Expedition of 1881 in Search of De Long and the* Jeannette. Boston: Houghton, Mifflin, 1917.

Nansen, Fridtjof. *Farthest North*. New York: Modern Library, 1999.

Newcomb, Raymond Lee, et al. *Our Lost Explorers: The Narrative of the* Jeannette *Expedition*. Hartford, CT: American Publishing, 1888.

Prentiss, Henry Mellen. *The Great Polar Current*. New York: Frederick A. Stokes, 1897.

Sides, Hampton. *In the Kingdom of Ice*. New York: Doubleday, 2014.

Vaughan, Richard. *The Arctic: A History*. Dover, NH: A. Sutton, 1994.

Williams, Henry Llewellyn. *History of the Adventurous Voyage and Terrible Shipwreck of the U.S. Steamer* Jeannette *in the Polar Seas*. New York: A. T. B. De Witt, 1882.

Government Documents

"Proceedings of a Court of Inquiry Convened at the Navy Department, Washington, D.C., October 5, 1882, in Pursuance of a Joint Resolution of Congress Approved August 8, 1882, to Investigate the Circumstances of the Loss in the Arctic Seas of the Exploring Steamer *Jeannette*, etc." Washington, DC: Government Printing Office, 1883.

"Report of Chief Engineer Geo. W. Melville in Connection with the *Jeannette* Expedition." Washington, DC: Government Printing Office, 1882.

"Report of Lieut. Jno. W. Danenhower in Connection with the *Jeannette* Expedition." Washington, DC: Government Printing Office, 1882.

Periodicals

Chicago Tribune. "The Fate of the *Jeannette*." February 18, 1880.

New York Evening Telegram. "Firm Belief in the Safety of the *Jeannette*." October 5, 1881.

New York Herald. "Arctic Exploration. Dr. Hayes on the Prospects of the *Jeannette*." July 31, 1880.

——. "The Arctic Mystery." January 20, 1879.

——. "Awful Calamity: The Wild Animals Broken Loose from Central Park." November 9, 1874.

——. "Brave Men's Fate: Bodies of *Jeannette*'s Crew Found Buried in Snow." June 27, 1882.

——. "The *Corwin*'s Cruise." June 20, 1880.

——. "De Long: Found Dead with His Party at the Lena's Mouth." May 6, 1882.

——. "From the *Jeannette*: Louis P. Noros Relates His Experience After He Left Captain De Long. . . ." April 20, 1882.

——. "The *Jeannette*: Continuation of Lieutenant Danenhower's Narrative." May 2, 1882.

——. "The *Jeannette*: Dr. Newcomb's Jottings About the Voyage." May 7, 1882.

——. "The *Jeannette*: The End of Lieutenant Danenhower's Story." May 5, 1882.

——. "The *Jeannette*: Engineer Melville's Account of the Ice Drift and Retreat." April 6, 1882.

——. "The *Jeannette*: Lieutenant Danenhower's Story of the Retreat." May 3, 1882.

——. "The *Jeannette*: Lost in the Arctic—Rescue of the Crew." December 21, 1881.

——. "The *Jeannette* Search: Engineer Melville at Yakutsk— His Sad Quest Ended." May 26, 1882.

——. "Wrangell Land Sighted." September 11, 1880.

New York Herald-Tribune. "Lone Survivor Recalls Terrors of Ill-Fated Quest for North Pole." January 8, 1928.

New York Times. "The Bennett Polar Expedition." May 23, 1878.

——. "Coffins Covered with Wreaths." February 22, 1884.

——. "De Long's Men on the Ice." October 24, 1882.

——."De Long's Tragic Death." November 22, 1882.

This flag pennant flew from the *Jeannette*'s main mast.

——. "From the Arctic Regions: The Return of Melville. . . ." September 14, 1882.

——. "The Ice Journey of the *Jeannette*'s Crew." October 25, 1882.

——. "In Capt. De Long's Boat." December 2, 1882.

——. "The *Jeannette* Wrecked." December 20, 1881.

——. "Mr. Bennett's Polar Schemes." July 22, 1878.

——. "Off for the Arctic Seas: Departure of the *Jeannette* from San Francisco." July 9, 1879.

——. "On the Siberian Coast." November 14, 1882.

——. "The Quarrels and Troubles on the *Jeannette*." November 24, 1882.

——. "The Retreat on the Ice." November 10, 1882.

——. "Seeking Aid for De Long." December 7, 1882.

——. "The Wreck of the *Jeannette*." January 9, 1882.

——. "The Wrecked Arctic Explorers." December 24, 1881.

This silk ribbon adorned a railroad car that carried the remains of the *Jeannette* expedition members out of Siberia.

Den Märtyrern
der
Jeanette - Expedition
in Anerkennung ihrer
heldenmüthigen Pflichttreue.

SOURCE NOTES

The source of each quotation in this book is indicated below. The citation provides the first words of the quotation and its document source. The sources are listed in the bibliography.

The following abbreviations are used:

Ambler (Gatewood: *The Private Journal of James Markham Ambler, M.D.*)
Court (*Proceedings of a Court of Inquiry . . .*)
Lena (Melville: *In the Lena Delta*)
Lost (Newcomb: *Our Lost Explorers*)
NYH (*New York Herald*)
Voyage (De Long: *The Voyage of the* Jeannette, Volumes 1 and 2)
Wife (E. De Long: *Explorer's Wife*)

JUNE 11, 1881: NORTH OF THE ARCTIC CIRCLE (page 10)
"Should success crown . . .": *New York Commercial Advertiser,* July 9, 1879, Guttridge, p. 3.

CHAPTER 1 (page 14)
"Awful Calamity . . ." and "Not one word . . .": NYH, November 9, 1874.
"the heroism of . . .": Wife, p. 88.
"tossed and tumbled": Voyage 1, p. 21.
"When the gale . . .": Ibid., p. 36.
"I felt pretty well . . .": Ibid., p. 32.
"was by far . . .": Wife, pp. 87–88.

CHAPTER 2 (page 21)

"great seclusion" and "shield him . . .": Voyage 1, pp. 1, 2.
"the incessant risks . . .": Ibid., p. 3.
"almost uncontrollable . . .": Ibid., p. 4.
"To me this . . ." through "Well, Midshipman . . .": Wife, pp. 9–10.
"dashing" and "adventurous spirit": Ibid., p. 3.
"I feel as though . . .": Ibid., p. 26.
"I had as strong . . .": Ibid., p. 3.
"My childhood . . .": Ibid., p. 13.
"armchair rover": Guttridge, p. 39.
"The central area . . .": Ibid., p. 40.
"worth his weight . . .": Hoehling, p. 16.
"the happiest period . . .": Wife, p. 119.
"Requirements for . . .": Voyage 1, p. 68.
"Our outfit is . . .": Ibid., p. 61.

CHAPTER 3 (page 30)

"I have been . . ." and "I shan't be . . .": Wife, pp. 159, 160.
"Good-by": Ibid., p. 163.
"as if I had . . .": Ibid., p 173.
"Pull away, men.": Ibid., p. 163.
"The docks were . . ." and "Telegraph Hill . . .": Ibid., pp. 164, 165.
"he might have . . .": Ibid., p. 150.
"He is not only . . .": Voyage 1, August 12, 1879, p. 91.
"I have been . . .": Wife, p. 172.
"as lovesick . . .": Ibid., p. 177.
"I could see . . .": Ibid., p. 173.
"If by any mischance . . .": Ibid., p. 177.
"Reached this place . . .": Ibid., p. 178.
"For the last two . . .": Ibid., p. 179.
"he vanished into . . .": Ibid., p. 189.
"We observe a . . .": Voyage 1, September 4, 1879.
"A clear and pleasant . . .": Ibid., September 5, 1879.
"While working along . . .": Court, p. 22.

CHAPTER 4 (page 40)

"As far as the . . ." and "This is a glorious . . .":
    Voyage 1, September 6, 1879.
"The whole pack . . .": Ibid., September 10, 1879.
"It is unpleasant . . .": Ibid., September 12, 1879.
"It was thought . . .": Lena, p. 8.
"no driftwood . . .": Voyage 1, September 14, 1879.

"Herald Island will . . .": Ibid.
"floe rats": Danenhower, p. 16.
"is very distant.": Voyage 1, September 19, 1879.
"We are securely . . .": Ibid., September 20, 1879.
"Our position was . . .": Danenhower, pp. 6–7.
"At three P. M. . . .": Voyage 1, October 3, 1879.
"At ten A. M. . . .": Ibid., October 5, 1879.
"We have now . . .": Ibid., October 17, 1879.
"[Alexey] and myself . . .": NYH, May 7, 1882.

CHAPTER 5 (page 47)
"Visions of pie . . .": NYH, May 7, 1882.
"a ten-cent plate . . .": Lena, p. 41.
"superior to any . . .": Voyage 1, November 6, 1879.
"beginning at a . . .": Ibid., March 16, 1880.
"As coal is . . .": Ibid., September 21, 1879.
"Melville has made . . .": Ibid., December 9, 1879.
"scooped up two . . .": Ibid., March 26, 1880.
"There can be . . .": Ibid., June 21, 1880.
"Here, Ninky . . .": Wife, p. 175.
"very buoyant . . .": NYH, May 7, 1882.
"These were the . . .": Ibid.
"Natural History is . . .": Voyage 1, May 17, 1880.
"Remove those birds.": De Long, quoted in Hoehling, p. 53.
Jeannette's Winter Schedule: Ibid., p. 50.
"Ice is in motion . . .":
    NYH, May 7, 1882.
"Were it not for . . .":
    Voyage 1, December 4, 1879.
"The necessary . . .":
    Ibid., December 9, 1879.
"Christmas Day!": Ibid.,
    December 25, 1879.

De Long's scissors

CHAPTER 6 (page 54)
"and Alexey gave . . ." and "the crew seemed . . .":
    Voyage 1, December 25, 1879.
"Arctic turkey": NYH, May 7, 1882.
"Our men had . . ." through "When, the performance . . .":
    Voyage 1, January 1, 1880.
"One day soon . . .": NYH, May 7, 1882.
"This morning . . .": Voyage 1, January 5, 1880.
"The carpenters . . .": Ibid., January 13, 1880.

CHAPTER 7 (page 57)

"but this horrible . . .": Voyage 1, January 15, 1880.
"I know of no . . .": Ibid., November 11, 1879.
"The ice was . . ." and "groaning and grinding":
     Ibid., January 19, 1880.
"With light hearts . . ." and "The temperature . . .": Lena, p. 13.
"Time meant . . .": Ibid., p. 14.
"As fast as he . . .": Voyage 1, January 19, 1880.
"as hard-working . . .": Wife, p. 176.
"for men cannot . . .": Voyage 1, January 19, 1880.
"We do not gain . . .": Ibid., January 20, 1880.
"Pumping by hand . . .": Ibid., February 5, 1880.
"the reappearance . . .": Ibid., January 26, 1880.
"At last we have . . .": Ibid., February 13, 1880.
"Verily, all . . .": Ibid., February 15, 1880.
"wretchedly wet . . .": Ibid., January 23, 1880.
"All our hoped . . .": Ibid., February 19, 1880.

CHAPTER 8 (page 63)

"triumphant news": NYH, July 31, 1880.
"the silly prophesies" and "perfectly confident . . .":
     Wife, pp. 191–92.
"The *Herald*'s . . .": Ibid., p. 192.
"letters to nowhere": Ibid., p. 190.
"I am well . . .": Ibid., p. 191.
"They did not go . . .": *Chicago Tribune*, February 18, 1880.
"Danenhower had . . .": Voyage 1, March 1, 1880.
"Although the sun . . .": Ibid., April 6, 1880.
"From aloft the . . .": Ibid., April 18, 1880.

CHAPTER 9 (page 67)

"They seem perfectly . . .": Voyage 1, June 23, 1880.
"much to the disgust . . ." and "We skinned him . . .": Ibid.,
     October 29, 1879.
"premature demise": Voyage 2, December 21, 1880, p. 494.
"came up from . . ." through "Ordinarily they . . .": Ibid.,
     March 6, 1881, pp. 523–24, 525.
"Chipp observed . . .": Voyage 1, April 30, 1880.
"Each day finds . . .": Ibid., May 7, 1880.
"As to there being . . .": Ibid., June 3, 1880.
"A day of almost . . .": Ibid., July 10, 1880.

CHAPTER 10 (page 73)

"winding and intricate": Voyage 1, August 22, 1880.
"Is this always . . ." through "It is hard to . . .": Ibid., August 17, 1880.
"which obliged me . . ." through "Lesson for me . . .": Ibid.,
    August 22, 1880.
"Shall we be . . ." and "In six additional . . .": Ibid., August 29, 1880.
"A cheerless and . . .": Voyage 2, September 2, 1880, p. 444.
"One year in . . .": Ibid., September 5, 1880, p. 445.
"At six A. M. . . .": Ibid., October 5, 1880, pp. 466–67.
"The snow would . . .": NYH, May 7, 1882.

CHAPTER 11 (page 79)

"dull and heavy . . .": Voyage 2, November 28, 1880, p. 491.
"a general want . . .": Ibid., November 3, 1880, p. 482.
"I am very much . . .": Ibid., September 19, 1880, pp. 454–55.
"Pemmican, bread . . .": Ibid., October 5, 1880, p. 467.
"poetical": Voyage 1, November 30, 1879.
"Imagine a moon . . .": Voyage 2, October 16, 1880, p. 472.
"we may feel . . .": Brooks, *Scientific Inferences*, p. 7.
"The day was made . . .": Voyage 2, December 25, 1880, p. 496.
"Melville and Dunbar . . .": Ibid., January 1, 1881, pp. 501–2.
"One year ago . . .": Ibid., January 19, 1881, p. 505.
"This year we . . .": Ibid., February 5, 1881, pp. 514–15.
"Another instance of . . .": Ibid., February 24, 1881, p. 521.
"This was our . . .": Lena, p. 15.
"The medical examination . . .": Voyage 2, March 1, 1881, p. 523.
"LAND! There is . . .": Ibid., May 16, 1881, pp. 544–45, 546.

CHAPTER 12 (page 86)

"thrown into chaotic . . .": Lost, p. 114.
"there was no . . .": and "The thermometers . . .": Lena, p. 17.
"It was cruel . . ." through "and made no . . .": Ibid., p. 18.
"The condition of . . .": Ibid., p. 17.
"the island at length . . ." and "great bodies of ice . . .": Ibid., p. 19.
"a dash for . . .": Ibid., p. 20.
"We waded and . . .": Ibid., p. 21.
"What next? The . . .": Voyage 2, June 1, 1881, pp. 558–59.
"Our lead invalids . . .": Ibid., June 2, 1881, p. 560.
"Nothing yet . . .": Ibid., June 3, 1881, p. 561.

CHAPTER 13 (page 91)

"Who shot the . . .": Lena, p. 16.
"What use is it . . .": Voyage 2, June 1, 1881, p. 560.
"which nestled . . .": Lena, p. 22.
"and dragged the . . ." and "From this time on . . .": Ibid., p. 23.
"Poor Nindemann . . ." through "Nindemann laughed . . .":
    Ibid., p. 24.
"crash! . . ." and "Stunned and . . .": Voyage 2, June 5, 1881.
"Well done . . .": Lena, p. 25.
"Thank God, we . . .": Voyage 2, June 5, 1881, p. 566.
"We were all . . .": Lena, p. 27.
"Lanes and openings . . .": Voyage 2, June 6, 1881, p. 567.
"We are leaving . . .": Ibid., June 8, 1881, p. 569.
"At four P. M. . . .": Ibid., June 11, 1881, p. 573.

CHAPTER 14 (page 96)

"jumped from . . .": Lost, p. 306.
"Well, what do . . ." and "She will either . . .": Lena, p. 28.
"Preparations had . . .": Ibid., p. 29.
"In fact . . .": Court, p. 92.
"Good by . . .": Lena, p. 30.
"beside the contents . . .": Voyage 2, June 12, 1881, p. 578.
"There she goes . . .": Court, p. 93.
"everybody seems . . .": Voyage 2, June 12, 1881, p. 578.
"tend to their . . .": Ibid., June 13, 1881, p. 579.
"honest Jacks": Lena, p. 31.
"And here we . . ." and "And thankful . . .": Ibid., pp. 30–31.

CHAPTER 15 (page 101)

"The clouds lifted . . .": Muir, p. 77.
"Of course . . .": Ibid., p. 33.
"may get somewhere": Voyage 2, June 17, 1881, p. 590.
"The clothing . . .": Ibid., June 15, 1881, p. 584.
"Breakfast . . .": Ibid., June 16, 1881, p. 587.
"Call all hands . . .": Ibid., p. 586.
"superhuman exertions": Ibid., June 17, 1881, p. 591.
"Twenty-eight men . . .": Ibid., June 18, 1881, p. 594.
"Aided by these . . .": Lena, p. 34.
"all hands were . . ." through "To make one . . .": Ibid., pp. 35–36.
"At no time . . .": Voyage 2, June 20, 1881, p. 597.
"I hardly had gone . . .": Ibid., June 22, 1881, p. 599.
"There is no work . . .": Ibid., June 24, 1881, p. 604.

CHAPTER 16 (page 108)

"If we go on . . .": De Long, quoted in Guttridge, p. 190.
"out of which . . .": Lena, pp. 38, 39.
"I generally get . . .": Ambler, July 14, 1881.
"The land stood . . .": Lena, p. 42.
"Look!": Voyage 2, July 28, 1881, p. 675.
"It infused new . . .": Lena, p. 43.
"were sweeping past . . ." through "waded, or jumped . . .":
   Voyage 2, July 28, 1881, pp. 675, 676, 679.
"sunburned, lean . . .": Hoehling, p. 98.
"And never were . . .": Voyage 2, July 28, 1881, p. 679.
"This is a magnificent . . .": Lost, p. 310.
"I notice the . . .": NYH, May 7, 1882.
"The amount of . . .": Voyage 2, August 5, 1881, p. 691.
"the rarest of . . .": Ibid., August 6, 1881, p. 693.
"to their utmost . . .": Ibid., August 7, 1881, p. 694.
"an excellent sea boat" and "a very bad . . .": Danenhower, pp. 59–60.
"From his very . . .": Ambler, August 14, 1881.
"Order to Melville. . . .": Voyage 2, August 7, 1881, pp. 696–97.
"First Cutter. Second . . .": Ibid., p. 694.
"the hardest morning's . . .": Ibid., September 4, 1881, p. 732.
"Dimly through . . .": Ibid., September 4, 1881, p. 735.
"The night was . . .": Lost, p. 318.
"This gave us a . . .": Voyage 2, September 10, 1881, p. 746.
"Captain . . .": Melville, quoted in Guttridge, p. 213.
"it was the last . . .": Lena, p. 61.

CHAPTER 17 (page 120)

"How can we . . ." through "Take charge!":
   attributed to Danenhower, p. 65.
"for dear life": Leach, quoted in Lost, p. 139.
"It seemed . . .": Lena, pp. 63, 64.
"a monstrous . . ." through "some message . . .": Ibid., p. 64.
"saw her far off . . ." through "I could discern . . .": Ibid., p. 65.
"What now?" and "Steer with the . . .":
   attributed to Danenhower, p. 66.
"ran in threes . . ." and "Lower away!" and "The boat came . . .":
   Ibid., p. 67.
"Everybody did his . . .": NYH, May 7, 1882.
"I sat at . . .": Leach, quoted in Lost, p. 139.
"which induced . . .": Lena, p. 72.

CHAPTER 18 (page 125)

"sodden and spongy": Lena, p. 83.

"We were wet . . .": NYH, May 7, 1882.

"we speculated . . .": Lena, p. 78.

"probably in a . . .": Danenhower, p. 71.

"roamed all over . . .": Lena, p. 75.

"as if millions . . .": Danenhower, p. 72.

"Bitterly we . . .": Melville, quoted in Guttridge, p. 235.

"to meet the . . ." and "to open up . . .": Lena, p. 88.

"In stature they . . .": Lost, p. 323.

"Cushat, cushat" through "pomree": Lena, pp. 89, 91.

"could barely . . .": Ibid., p. 97.

"the dirty, crumpled . . ." and "Arctic steamer . . .": Ibid., p. 144.

CHAPTER 19 (page 130)

"a nervous . . .": Ambler, September 18, 1881.

"The following named . . .": Voyage 2, September 19, 1881, p. 756.

"hobbled along . . ." and "Every one of us . . .":
    Ibid., September 20, 1881, p. 757.

"look very bad . . .": Ambler, September 27, 1881.

"I cannot go . . .": attributed to Nindemann, Court, p. 180.

"no man will be . . .": Ambler, September 28, 1881.

"concluded that . . ." through "The darkest . . .": Voyage 2,
    September 21, 1881, pp. 763, 764, 765.

"Meat free from . . .": Ibid., September 23, 1881, p. 767.

"as a surprise . . .": Ibid., September 24, 1881.

"and the dog": Ibid., September 26, 1881, p. 770.

"Saved again!": Ibid., September 27, 1881, p. 771.

"I had nothing . . ." and "I saw some toes . . .": Court, p. 188.

"departed this life . . .": Voyage 2, October 6, 1881, p. 790.

"The seaman's grave . . .": attributed to Nindemann, Court, p. 191.

"In Memory": Voyage 2, October 6, 1881, p. 791.

"Peace to his soul.": Ambler, October 6, 1881.

"Nindemann, do you . . ." and "He told me. . .": attributed to
    Nindemann, Court, p. 191.

"get over ground . . .": Hoehling, p. 129.

"If you find . . .": attributed to Nindemann, Court, p. 194.

"a high, conical . . .": Lost, p. 137.

"Eat deerskin . . .": Voyage 2, October 10, 1881, pp. 795, 796.

"S. W. gale . . .": Ibid., October 11, 1881, p. 796.

"For dinner . . .": Ibid., October 12, 1881.

"We are in the . . .": Ibid., October 13, 1881.

CHAPTER 20 (page 141)

"Exhaustion from . . .": Ambler, October 18, 1881.
"prayers for . . .": Voyage 2, October 21, 1881, p. 797.
"Suffering in . . .": Ibid., October 23, 1881, p. 800.
"A hard night": Ibid., October 24, 1881.
"Noros now and . . .": Court, p. 198.
"that we were . . .": Noros, quoted in Lost, p. 135.
"This was always . . .": Court, p. 201.
"a lot of huts . . ." and "commandant": Court, p. 208.
"At Bulun we . . .": Noros, quoted in Lost, p. 135.
"dirty and miserable" and "On the evening of . . .": Court, p. 210.
"Hello, Noros . . .": Ibid., p. 211.

CHAPTER 21 (page 145)

"Both were so . . .": Lena, p. 165.
"vigorous and constant . . .": Melville, quoted in Guttridge, p. 261.
"Soak, soak" through "Cushat soak": Lena, pp. 184, 185.
"They explained . . .": Melville, quoted in Hoehling, p. 141.
"And after they . . .": Ibid., p. 139.
"I was now so . . .": Lena, p. 188.
"deer bones with . . .": Ibid., p. 187.
"until I found . . .": Melville, quoted in Guttridge, p. 264.
"The natives were . . .": Lena, p. 221.
"Omit no . . .": Ibid., p. 276.
"off the record": Guttridge, p. 273.
"Commander De Long . . .": Ibid., p. 274.
"If George was . . .": Wife, p. 205.
"It seems so . . .": Ibid., p. 276.

De Long's whistle was useful for getting the crew's attention.

"entirely misled me": Ibid., p. 206.
"raised false hopes": Bennett, quoted in Guttridge, p. 275.
"After cleaving her . . .": Hoehling, p. 147.
"All this forms . . .": Wife, p. 206.

CHAPTER 22 (page 152)
"To the southward . . .": Lena, p. 284.
"I caught sight . . ." and "He lay on . . .": Ibid., p. 331.
"Mr. Collins dying": Voyage 2, October 30, 1881, p. 800.
"There he kept . . .": Lena, p. 335.
"I write these lines . . .": Ambler, pp. 58-59.
"he firmly believed . . ." and "No doubt the . . .": Wife, p. 219.
"I have found . . .": Hoehling, p. 167.

CHAPTER 23 (page 159)
"We want Melville!": *New York Times*, September 14, 1882.
"It was as if . . .": Wife, p. 220.
"I will stand . . .": Melville, quoted in Ibid., p. 225.
"I feel that . . .": Melville, quoted in Lost, p. 476.
"On the day . . ." through "Finally, arriving . . .":
    Lena, pp. 393, 394, 395, 396.

EPILOGUE (page 165)
"seems to have been . . .": Court, p. 266.
"If men must . . .": Melville, quoted in
    Guttridge, p. 328.

INDEX

Page numbers in **boldface** refer to images and/or captions.

A

Ah Sam, 5, 34, 116, 131, 141, 154, **154**, 157
Alexey, 5, 35, **37**, 41–42, 44, 46, 54, 55–56, 67, 84, 99, **100**, 101, 116, 117, 131, 135–136, **136**, 139, 141, 152, 157, **166**, 167, 171–172
Ambler, James M., 5, 32, 48, 62, 79, 83, 84, 90, 91, **91**, 94, 108–109, 115, 116, 130, 131, 134–135, 138–139, 141, 149, 154–157, **156**
Aneguin, 5, 35, **37**, 44, 46, 55, 116, **150**, **166**, 167, 171–172
Arctic Ocean, **2**, 11, 109, 168
Arthur, Chester A., 160

B

Bartlett, James H., 5, 87, 116, 146, 148, 149, **150**, 152, 157, **157**
Bennett, James Gordon, Jr., 16–20, **18**, 24, 26, 28, 29, 31, 62, 63–64, 87, 92, 101, 148–149, 151, 159, 161
Bennett Island, **2**, 111, **112–113**, 115, **126**, 168
Bering Strait, **2**, 25, 37
Boyd, George W., 5, 116, 131, 141, **154**, **156**
Bulun, **2**, 128–129, 144, 146, 148–149, 152

C

California Academy of Sciences, 81
Canandaigua, 23
Cape Barkin, Russia, 125
Cape Emma, 111, 115
Central Park Zoo, 16
Chicago Tribune, 64
Chipp, Charles W., 5, 28, 33, 41–42, **42**, 48, 71, 78, 98, 99, 105, 107, 114, 116, 122–123, 127, 158, 159
Civil War, 18, 22, 23, 34, 163
Cole, John "Jack," 5, 28, 29, 54–55, 62, 110, 116, 123, **150**
Collins, Jerome, 5, 32–33, 34, 55, **55**, 62, 116, 131, 141, 154, **154**, 155, **156**, 157, 160, 166

D

Danenhower, John W., 5, 32, 39, 43, 56, 60, 62, **62**, 64, 65, 84, 98, 99, **100**, 107, 109, 114–116, 121–123, 125, 148–149, **150**, 165–166
De Long, Emma, 23–24, **25**, 26, 28, 30, 31, 34–35, **36**, 38, 64, 111, 151, 154, 156–157, 160–161, 167
De Long, George W., 5, **17**, **27**, **100**, **130**, **133**, **136**, **137**, **156**, **158**, **171**, **172**, **179**, **185**

bear encounter, 73–76, **75**
Canandaigua, 23
childhood and
  adolescence, 21–22
death, 153, **153, 154, 156,**
  158, **158**
funeral, **165**, 167
Juniata and *Little Juniata*,
  18–21
orders to crew and officers,
  11, 28, 51, 52, 103–104,
  115–116, 125, 151
relationship with
  Alexey, 35, 41, 44, 67,
    84, 99, 135–136, 139
  Ambler, 32, 108, 109,
    115, 130, 135, 141
  Aneguin, 35, 44
  Bennett, 16, 18–19, 24,
    26, 29
  Chipp, 28, 33, 41, 71, 78,
    99, 107
  Collins, 32–33, 62, 154
  Danenhower, 32, 56, 60,
    65, 84, 99, 107, 109, 115,
    149, 165
  De Long, Emma,
    23–24, 30–31, 34–35,
    36, 38, 73, 111, 151,
    154, 156–157, 161, 167
  De Long, Sylvie, 24, 35,
    154, **154**
  Dunbar, 83, 97, 105
  Ericksen, 135, 137, 138
  Melville, 34, 45, 49–50,
    83, 94, 107, 108,
    115–116, 118–119, 122,
    125, 145–149, **146,**
    153, 153–158, 160–162
  Newcomb, 33, 51
  Nindemann, 59, 135,
    138, 139, 167

  U.S. Naval Academy,
    22–23, **22**
De Long, Sylvie, 24, **25**, 26, 28,
  35, 154, **154**
dogs of the *Jeannette*, 12, 35,
  41, **44, 45,** 51, 67–71, **68–69,**
  70, 71, 76, 87–88, 92, 96, 105,
  107, 111, **112,** 116–117, 135,
  136, 138
Dressler, Adolph, 5, 116, 131,
  141, **154**
Dunbar, William, 5, 33, **33,** 41,
  83, 84, 86, 87, 89, 92–93, 97,
  105, 116

E

Edison, Thomas, 33, 160
Eremoff, Kusmah, 129
Ericksen, Hans H., 5, 87, 89,
  92–93, 116, 131, 134–139, 151, 157
Explorer's Wife, 167

F

Fall River, MA, 167
Fram, 168
Franklin, John, 16

G

Garfield, James A., 160
Görtz, Carl A., 5, 116, 131, 141,
  154, 156
Greenland, 19, 26, 38, 87, 101, 168

H

Hayes, Isaac, 63, **63**
Hayes, Rutherford B., 160
Henrietta Island, **2,** 87–89, 92,
  95, **126,** 134, 168

Henson, Matthew, 169
Herald Island, **2**, 38, 40–43, 74

I

Irkutsk, Russia, 146, **158**
Iversen, Nelse, 5, 116, 131, 141, **154**, **156**

J

Jeannette, **8–9**, **10**, **40**, **44**, **55**, **61**, **63**, **132**, **137**, **150**, **175**
    damage to, 57–62, 78, 95
    as *Pandora*, 26, **40**
    preparations for voyage, 26–29
    sinking of, **2**, **3**, **9**, 11–12, 96–100, **96**, **100**, 102, **126**, 157
Jeannette Island, **2**, 84–85, **86**, 87, **126**, 168
Johnson, Peter E., 5, 116
Juniata, 19

K

Kaack, Heinrich H., 5, 116, 131, 141, **156**
Kuehne, Albert G., 5, 54–55, 90, 116
Kuro Siwo current, 24–25, 72, 87

L

Lauterbach, John, 5, 116, **150**
Leach, Herbert W., 5, 116, 122–124, **150**
Lee, Walter, 5, 116, 131, 140, 141, **156**, 163
Lena Delta, **126**, **130**, 131, 146, 155, 158, **158**, 164, 170–171

Lena River, **2**, 100, 114, 116, 125–127, **126**, 131
Little Juniata, 19–21, 28
Livingstone, David, 17

M

Mansen, Frank E., 5, 116, **150**
Melville, George W., 5, 31, **31**, 33, 34, 41–42, 44, 45, 48, 49–50, 58–60, 83, 84, 86–90, **86**, 92–93, 94, 96–100, **100**, 106–110, 114–116, 118–119, 121–124, 125–129, 130, 134, 144–149, **146**, **150**, 152–158, **153**, **157**, 159–164, 166, 167, 169
Muir, John, 101

N

Nansen, Fridtjof, 168
National Oceanic and Atmospheric Association (NOAA), 169
Nelson, Edward W., 35, 101
Newcomb, Raymond L., 5, 33–34, 44, 46, 47, **47**, 50–51, **51**, 53, 55, **76**, 78, 90, 97, 99, 111, 116, 117, 124, 125, 127–128, **150**, 166, 167, 169
New Siberian Islands, **2**, 94, 102, 114, **126**
New York Commercial Advertiser, 13
New York Evening Telegram, 159
New York Herald, 16–20, 25, 32, 55, 62, 63, **63**, 64, 92, 146, 148, 149, 151, 158, **158**, 159, 161
New York Times, 159
Nindemann, William F. C., 5, 58–59, **60**, 70–71, 87, 89, 93, 116, 129, 131, 134–136,

138–139, **142**, 143–152, **150**, **153**, 157, **157**, 159, 162, 167
Nordenskjöld, Adolf Erik, 37
Noros, Louis P., 5, 102, 116, 129, 131, 139, **142**, **143**, 143–145, 147–148, **150**, 151–152, 159, 162, 166–167, 168
North Bulun, Russia, 134
North Pole, **2**, 12, 14, 18–19, 24, 26, 37, 62, 63, 72, 77, 79, 165, 168

P

Pandora, 26, **40**
Parthia, 159–160
Peary, Robert, 169
Petermann, August, 24–26, 28, 35, 38, 49, 87, 114, 125, 127, 134
Plug Ugly, 67, 71, **71**
Polaris, 19

R

Rodgers, 101

S

Sagastyr, Russia, 134
Semenovski Island, **126**, 131
Sharvell, Walter, 5, 87, 116
Siberia, **2**, 25, 26, 32, 37, 66, 77, 80, 99, 101, 102, 106, 114, 116, 125, **126**, 128, 129, 146, **146**, 148, **150**, 151, 152, 157, 161, 163–165, 167, **171**, **176**
Snoozer, 67, 71, 111, 117, 135, 138
Stanley, Henry, 17
Starr, Edward, 5, 116
Stefansson, Vilhjalmur, 170
St. Michael, AK, 5, 35, **37**, 171

Sweetman, Alfred, 5, 28, 54, 59, 111, 116, 163

T

Thetis, 162, 164
Thomas Corwin, 101
Tomat, 128–129
Tong Sing, Charles, 5, 90, 116, **150**

U

Unalaska Island, 35

V

Vega, 32, 36–37, 41
von Wrangel, Ferdinand, 26

W

Warren, Henry D., 5, 116
Wilson, Henry, 5, 116, **150**
Wrangel Land, **2**, 26, 38, 81, 87

Y

Yakutsk, Russia, **2**, 146, 148–149, **150**

PICTURE CREDITS

Dartmouth College Rauner Special Collections Library: 63, 132–133, 158.

Library of Congress: *The New York Herald* (New York [NY]), 09 July 1879. *Chronicling America: Historic American Newspapers* (page 3): 4.

The Providence Athenæum: 14–15.

Voyage of the Jeannette, **Volume 1**
37, 43, 45, 70, 75; from a design by M. J. Burns, engraved by George T. Andrew: 44, 68–69; sketches by Raymond Lee Newcomb: 51, 71, 76.

Voyage of the Jeannette, **Volume 2**
61, 118, 126, 136, 156, 157; from a design by Captain Gronbeck, engraved by George T. Andrew: 153; from a design by M. J. Burns, engraved by George T. Andrew: Front Cover, 4, 8–9, 112, 120–121, 130, 142, 146; sketch by George W. Melville, 86.

Courtesy of the U.S. Naval Academy Museum, Annapolis, MD
3, 10, 17, 18, 22, 25 (left and right), 27, 31, 33, 36, 40, 42, 47, 55, 60, 62, 91, 96–97, 100 (painting by George Louis Poilleux-Saint-Ange), 137, 143, 150, 154 (bottom), 165 (bottom); Photos by Grant Walker: 154 (top), 165 (top), 166 (all), 171, 172, 173 (all), 175, 177, 185.

Sandra Neil Wallace had a lengthy career as a news anchor and ESPN sportscaster before writing realistic fiction and nonfiction for young readers. A journalism pioneer, she was the first woman to cover the National Hockey League on network TV. She is the author of the Orbis-Pictus Award-winning picture book biography, *Between the Lines*.

Rich Wallace has written more than 3 dozen novels for children and teens. His first novel, *Wrestling Sturbridge*, was selected by the American Library Association as one of the top 100 YA books of the 20th century.

Sandra and Neil also write books together. They are the coauthors of *Babe Conquers the World*; *The Teachers March!*, an Orbis Pictus Honor Book; and *Race Against Time*, an ALA Notable Book. Visit sandraneilwallace.com and richwallacebooks.com.